D1572569

LIVING

❖ THE ❖

BOOK OF MORMON

LIVING

 THE ❖

BOOK OF MORMON

A GUIDE TO UNDERSTANDING
AND APPLYING ITS PRINCIPLES
IN TODAY'S WORLD.

ALLAN K. BURGESS

BOOKCRAFT
Salt Lake City, Utah

Copyright © 1991 by Bookcraft, Inc.

All rights reserved. No part of this book may be reproduced in any form or by any means without permission in writing from the publisher, Bookcraft, Inc., 1848 West 2300 South, Salt Lake City, Utah 84119.

Bookcraft is a registered trademark of Bookcraft, Inc.

Library of Congress Catalog Card Number: 91–75417
ISBN 0–88494–802–1

First Printing, 1991

Printed in the United States of America

To my 1990–91 seminary students

CONTENTS

PREFACE

Many people study the scriptures conscientiously but never come to an understanding of the truth. One man even memorized, word for word, the whole Gospel of Matthew, but his understanding of the doctrine was very shallow. Just studying the scriptures does not guarantee spiritual growth or greater understanding and comprehension. Learning the word of God is different from other kinds of learning.

We will never come to know the Lord and understand the truths of the gospel simply by setting a goal to gain knowledge. An important principle that directs gospel learning is that we need to desire to *be* true, not just to *find* truth. Those who receive the promised blessings of scripture study do not just search for information; they search for concepts that can be applied in their lives so they can better do what God wants them to do.

When we approach scripture study with the goal of gospel application in mind, God blesses us with his Spirit and opens up the scriptures to our understanding. Nephi said that he likened all scripture to his people, that it might be for their profit and learning (see 1 Nephi 19:23). Jesus said, "If any man will do [God's] will, he shall know of the doctrine" (John 7:17). When we immerse ourselves in the scriptures with the desire to apply what we learn, we receive a much deeper understanding and witness of the eternal truths found there than when we merely read to learn facts. God, through the scriptures and the Holy Ghost, then speaks to us personally.

This book has been written and arranged with these concepts in mind. Instead of just zeroing in on the doctrine or history of the Book of Mormon, the book identifies and discusses important verses that can be pondered and applied in our lives today. Of course, you will see other applications of some of these verses that may be more important to you than the ones discussed. As you apply the truths in these verses, the result will be a better understanding of the Book of Mormon and of the will of God. You will also find much joy and happiness, because your capacity to live the gospel and a Christ-like life will increase.

ACKNOWLEDGMENTS

I am indebted to my 1990–91 seminary students, who were a great inspiration to me. Our course of instruction was the Book of Mormon, and these students showed a great desire to study that book of scripture and make its teachings part of their lives. Most of them studied the Book of Mormon daily during their personal study time at home, and several times during the week they shared many of their favorite scriptures with other class members.

Many of these students already have strong testimonies and, at their young ages, have come to love the Lord and dedicate their lives to him. The love they have shown to both God and me has increased the love that I feel for others, for the Savior, and for our Father in Heaven. Because of them, my own dedication and commitment to gospel living have increased. It has been a humbling experience to teach young people who are so willing and eager to learn the truth and do what is right. Their love for the Savior and for fellow classmates has been a great example for me. I have come to love them very much, and I pray that they will always feel the enthusiasm for the Book of Mormon that they feel now.

Chapter 1

MANY AFFLICTIONS
BUT HIGHLY FAVORED

1 NEPHI 1–2

Both Lehi and Nephi endured many afflictions in their lives. They left their comfortable home and departed into the wilderness, where they lived for eight years. Prior to that, the people of Jerusalem had mocked Lehi and tried to take his life. Nephi was constantly mocked and ridiculed by his older brothers and other relatives and came close to being murdered on at least five different occasions. Four of these threats to his life came from his own brothers. Yet we find both Lehi and Nephi sharing feelings of gratitude to the Lord for the greater blessings he had given them.

After Lehi had left Jerusalem and all of his worldly possessions and comforts behind, the following incident took place. "And it came to pass that when he had traveled three days in the wilderness, he pitched his tent in a valley by the side of a river of water. And it came to pass that he built an altar of stones, and made an offering unto the Lord, and gave thanks unto the Lord our God." (1 Nephi 2:6–7.)

Nephi seemed to be just as appreciative of the Lord as his father was. He started his record of God's dealings with his family in this way: "I Nephi, having been born of goodly parents, therefore I was taught somewhat in all the learning of my father; and having seen many afflictions in the course of my days, nevertheless, having been highly favored of the Lord in all my days; yea, having had a great knowledge of the goodness and the mysteries of God, therefore I make a record of my proceedings in my days" (1 Nephi 1:1).

Nephi's ability to recognize and appreciate the Lord and his blessings in spite of his many afflictions can be a great example to all of us. Often we allow ourselves to be caught up and even overwhelmed in our problems and challenges while we overlook the great love God has shown us and the great blessings he has bestowed upon us. Some of these blessings are priceless—such as the atonement of Jesus Christ, a personal testimony as to gospel truths, the scriptures, the opportunity to pray, and the tremendous gift of agency.

It is easy to look around and think that someone else's circumstances are preferable to our own, and to become blinded to the great blessings we do have. We sometimes feel resentful because others seem to have easier lives, more money, or better health, or they seem smarter or more personable than we are. Elder Henry D. Moyle said something that should help all of us feel more content with the challenges we face and the circumstances we find ourselves in:

> I believe that we . . . might well take to heart the admonition of Alma and be content with that which God hath allotted us. We might well be assured that we had something to do with our "allotment" in our pre-existent state. This would be an additional reason for us to accept our present condition and make the best of it. It is what we agreed to do.
>
> . . . We unquestionably knew before we elected to come to this earth the conditions under which we would here exist, and live, and work. So little wonder it is that Alma of old said that we sin in the thought, or in the desire, or in the wish that we were someone other than ourselves. (*Improvement Era*, December 1952, p. 934.)

Margaret and Bud are a married couple who have "seen many afflictions" yet been "highly favored of the Lord." Their first child, a daughter, was born malformed, missing parts of her arms and legs. When their second child was born they counted his fingers and toes, but his was another problem. They soon found that he had cystic fibrosis, his life expectancy being two years. Their third child was strong and healthy and has become the mother of their six grandchildren. Their fourth baby lived only eight days; Margaret got to hold him once.

Looking back on the challenges that they had faced, Margaret said: "We found that we were never alone—always there was the Spirit, guiding, comforting, supporting us from day to day, through the good news and bad. We came to marvel at the peace that 'passeth understanding.' As a young married couple the first thing we learned was that these kinds of tragedies bring hardships. They bring sorrow and grief and heartbreak. But although we wept many tears, we were surprised to find that *we were still happy!* Even death, the event we fear most, only intensifies the joy gleaned from the knowledge that not only will we live again but we will live again as families."

Very few of us wrestle with afflictions that are so serious or so numerous as the ones Lehi, Nephi, Margaret, and Bud faced, yet all of us can share in the blessings that are available from the Lord. Every one of us, if we take the time to evaluate and ponder our lives, can say, "I have seen many afflictions in the course of my days, nevertheless, I have been highly favored of the Lord in all my days!" It would be a good idea to reinforce our gratitude by not letting a prayer go by without thanking God for his goodness and mercy.

Chapter 2

KNEW NOT THE
DEALINGS OF GOD

1 NEPHI 2, 15

Laman and Lemuel murmured and complained constantly, even after they were visited by an angel. Lehi was very worried about them and told them he wished they would be righteous, firm, and steadfast, but they were upset because they had to leave their home and wealth. They did not believe that Lehi was a prophet and felt they would perish in the wilderness. A key to their spiritual weakness and constant murmuring is given in the following verse: "And thus Laman and Lemuel, being the eldest, did murmur against their father. And they did murmur because they knew not the dealings of that God who had created them." (1 Nephi 2:12.)

Why didn't Laman and Lemuel know the dealings of God? Why didn't they believe that their father was a prophet? We know that God wants everyone to respond to his prophets and recognize his dealings, so what kept Laman and Lemuel in spiritual darkness? The answers to these questions can be found in 1 Nephi 15. Nephi writes: "And I said unto them: Have ye inquired of the Lord? And they said unto me: We have not; for the Lord maketh no such thing known unto us. Behold, I said unto them: How is it that ye do not keep the commandments of the Lord? How is it that ye will perish, because of the hardness of your hearts? Do ye not remember the things which the Lord has said?—If ye will not harden your hearts, and ask me in faith, believing that ye shall receive, with diligence in keeping my commandments, surely these things shall be made known unto you." (1 Nephi 15:8–11.)

Laman and Lemuel did not receive personal witnesses of Lehi's calling and his teachings because they did not want to know the truth enough to pray and live for it. They preferred to believe that their father was not a prophet and that God did not want them to leave their home and riches and live in the wilderness. They made little effort to find or understand the truth.

Nephi and Sam were just the opposite. They not only desired to know that Lehi was a prophet but they also wanted to understand for themselves the things he taught, so they could better apply them in their lives. Nephi described the great desires he had to understand and live the gospel:

> And it came to pass that I, Nephi, being exceedingly young, nevertheless being large in stature, and also having great desires to know of the mysteries of God, wherefore, I did cry unto the Lord; and behold he did visit me, and did soften my heart that I did believe all the words which had been spoken by my father; wherefore, I did not rebel against him like unto my brothers. . . .
>
> And it came to pass that the Lord spake unto me, saying: Blessed art thou, Nephi, because of thy faith, for thou hast sought me diligently, with lowliness of heart.
>
> And inasmuch as ye shall keep my commandments, ye shall prosper. (1 Nephi 2:16, 19–20.)

Notice some of the key phrases that describe why Nephi came to know God's will and, therefore, did not murmur against his father. Some of these phrases are "desires to know," "cry unto the Lord," "sought diligently," and "lowliness of heart." Each of these phrases indicates the deep feelings and strong effort that Nephi put into knowing and applying the truth. He found the truth because he wanted, with all of his heart, to be true.

Elder Gene R. Cook said that "we do not desire blind obedience in the Church. We desire that every individual may know for himself that the counsel he receives from his leaders comes from the Lord. He has the right and the great privilege to know for himself of the Lord that he has been counseled aright." (*Ensign*, May 1978, p. 65.)

If we find ourselves murmuring constantly about decisions that are made by the Church leaders, it may be evidence that we have allowed ourselves to become more like Laman and Lemuel, and less like Nephi and Sam. It may be a sign to us that we are not praying, studying, and living the gospel with the enthusiasm that Nephi did. The next time we find ourselves murmuring about something our leaders are doing, we might ask ourselves, "Have I inquired of the Lord, and am I diligently keeping the commandments?"

Chapter 3

HE SHALL PREPARE A WAY

1 NEPHI 3:5–7

M ost Church leaders, if asked, could easily come up with a list of common reasons members have given them for not accepting a specific Church assignment or calling. Here are some of the familiar excuses:

"I just don't relate to teenagers."

"I was never meant to be a teacher—I can't think well when I stand up in front of people."

"I'm simply not a religious person. I don't feel comfortable in church."

"I just can't pray in front of people. I become all tongue-tied and can't think of anything to say."

"I'm more of a behind-the-scenes type of person. It is too hard for me to try to express myself to others."

"Being a clerk seems very boring. My qualifications are in other areas."

All of these excuses, and many others, might be summed up by saying, "What you want me to do is hard, and I don't want to do it"; or "I don't feel that I have the qualifications to do the job, and I don't have enough faith in God to believe he will help me succeed."

Laman and Lemuel were found constantly saying, "We can't," or "We don't want to," or "It is too hard." Laman and Lemuel did not understand that God will never ask us to do anything we cannot do. Nephi, on the other hand, realized that God would never ask him to do something and then leave him alone to fail.

The statement in 1 Nephi 3:7 is possibly the most often-quoted verse from the Book of Mormon. It appears in the context of Lehi's asking his sons to return to Jerusalem and obtain the brass plates from Laban. What Lehi is asking his sons to do is a hard thing. They have already traveled from Jerusalem to somewhere near the Red Sea, most of the journey being through a barren wilderness—a hot and dry wilderness that was plagued with marauders. They are being asked to make a return trip that will last for many days, obtain the plates, and spend many more strenuous days traveling back through the wilderness.

The man they are to get the plates from is wicked, cruel, short tempered, and greedy, and commands at least fifty soldiers or guards. Most of us—even Scoutmasters!—have not received an assignment that is quite this uncomfortable. In the face of this difficult request from the Lord, Lehi and Nephi teach us some great things about responding to calls from the Lord:

> And now, behold thy brothers murmur, saying it is a hard thing which I have required of them; but behold I have not required it of them, but it is a commandment of the Lord.
>
> Therefore go, my son, and thou shalt be favored of the Lord, because thou has not murmured.
>
> And it came to pass that I, Nephi, said unto my father: I will go and do the things which the Lord hath commanded, for I know that the Lord giveth no commandments unto the children of men, save he shall prepare a way for them that they may accomplish the thing which he commandeth them. (1 Nephi 3:5–7.)

Just as paying tithing or praying for family members that are ill are matters of faith, accepting Church callings and assignments also involves faith. God is our Father. He loves us and knows our strengths and weaknesses better than we do. As we strive to help his other children and to build his kingdom, he will not let us down.

The Lord said: "If men come unto me I will show unto them their weakness. I give unto men weakness that they may be humble; and my grace is sufficient for all men that humble themselves before me; for if they humble themselves before me, and have faith in me, then will I make weak things become strong unto them." (Ether 12:27.)

The truth of this scripture was manifest in the life of a young man named Phil. Phil was so shy that he felt absolutely petrified at the thought of speaking in front of others. As a senior in high school he was required to take a speech class. He was so afraid of speaking that the teacher told him she would give him an A if he would simply come to class every day and write a speech each week. When Phil got to college he had to take another speech class. It was the only class Phil ever received a failing grade in.

Because of the absolute terror he felt as he thought about giving talks in church and telling people about the gospel, for over three years Phil put off serving a mission. Finally, with the encouragement of a good bishop, Phil sincerely prayed to the Lord and received the strength to accept a mission call.

The first time Phil knocked on a door he was so frightened that he forgot his name and the name of the Church, but as he started to bear his testimony, the Spirit of the Lord penetrated the innermost depths of his heart and soul. By the end of the first day of his mission, with the Lord's help, his weakness was quickly becoming one of his strengths.

Phil is now a full-time seminary teacher, and he spends much of his time speaking at firesides, education weeks, and at Church meetings. People often tell Phil that he is a natural-born teacher, not realizing the great effect the Lord has had in Phil's life. Many lives, including Phil's, have been touched because he had enough faith to accept a call to serve the Lord.

When we realize that the person who created this earth and everything on it has committed all of his power, knowledge, and resources to helping us succeed, we can move forward with faith in him and do the things that he asks us to do. Elder Neal A. Maxwell summarized it well when he said, "God does not begin by asking us about our ability, but only about availability, and if we then prove our dependability, he will increase our capability!" (*Ensign*, July 1975, p. 7.)

Chapter 4

NOT KNOWING BEFOREHAND

1 NEPHI 4:6

Obtaining the brass plates from Laban was not an easy chore. Laman was the first to go to Laban, and in the end he had to run for his life. The brothers then gathered up all of their riches and tried to buy the plates, but they had to hide in a cave to avoid being killed. Nephi made the third attempt to obtain the plates. Because God had asked him to get the plates, he knew that God would prepare a way.

His brothers hid outside the city, and Nephi entered the city alone. The plan he followed not only worked for him but will work for us every day of our lives. Nephi wrote, "And I was led by the Spirit, not knowing beforehand the things which I should do" (1 Nephi 4:6).

Nephi did not sit around the cave waiting until the Lord revealed a foolproof plan before he went after the plates. He had done everything he could, and he knew that the Spirit would guide him as he tried to do what God had asked him to do. He also knew that God would not guide his mind and heart until he moved his feet.

Pondering this one short verse can lead us to some precious truths. Sometimes we need to step beyond our knowledge into the realm of faith. Elder Boyd K. Packer said: "Somewhere in your quest for spiritual knowledge, there is that 'leap of faith,' as the philosophers call it. It is the moment when you have gone to the *edge of the light and stepped into the darkness* to discover that the way is lighted ahead for just a footstep or two. 'The spirit of man,' as the scripture says, indeed 'is the candle of the Lord' (Proverbs 20:27)." (*Ensign*, January 1983, p. 54, italics added.)

This is the way it was for Nephi. He went to the edge of the light, stepped into the darkness, and found that the Spirit was there to show him the way.

There may be many reasons why God does not want us to see too far in front of us. One reason might be that we came to this earth to learn and develop so that, someday, we can become gods. God's full-time work is helping and directing us, with this end in mind (see Moses 1:39). If he doesn't give us enough help, we will fail. If he gives us too much help, we will become spiritually, emotionally, and intellectually dependent upon him, and our growth toward godhood will be limited. We have to learn to think and ponder and make proper decisions if we are to someday direct worlds of our own.

We need the help and influence and guidance of God, but we also need to work hard to overcome the challenges and obstacles that we face. The Lord told Oliver Cowdery: "Behold, you have not understood; you have supposed that I would give it unto you, when you took no thought save it was to ask me. But, behold, I say unto you, that you must study it out in your mind; then you must ask me if it be right, and if it is right I will cause that your bosom shall burn within you; therefore, you shall feel that it is right."(D&C 9:7–8.)

During the welfare session of the April 1978 general conference, Elder Packer gave a tremendous talk that addressed this very subject. He first talked about physical welfare and emphasized the importance of members of the Church doing *all that they can* for themselves before they are helped through the Church's welfare program. He then said that the same principle of self-reliance applies spiritually and emotionally as well. He was concerned about the amount of counseling being doled out by priesthood leaders and went on to say:

> We seem to be developing an epidemic of "counselitis" which drains spiritual strength from the Church, much like the common cold drains more strength out of humanity than any other disease.

That, some may assume, is not serious. It is very serious!

On one hand, we counsel bishops to avoid abuses in welfare help. On the other hand, some bishops dole out counsel and advice without considering that the member should solve the problem himself. . . .

If we lose our emotional and spiritual independence, our self-reliance, we can be weakened quite as much, perhaps even more, than when we become dependent materially.

If we are not careful, we can lose the power of individual revelation. . . .

Spiritual independence and self-reliance is a sustaining power in the Church. If we rob the members of that, how can they get revelation for themselves? How will they know there is a prophet of God? How can they get answers to prayers? How can they know for *sure* for themselves? (*Ensign*, May 1978, pp. 91–92, italics in original.)

These same principles hold true in our relationship with our Father in Heaven. He wants us to listen to and follow the Spirit. He wants us to seek his counsel and appreciate his help. But he wants us to do all that we can do for ourselves, using our own talents and intellect. He doesn't want us to sit around and wait for revelation before we will take up our cross and follow him. Many times in our lives we will be expected to walk to the edge of the light and step into the darkness before he will show us the way. Then we will be like Nephi who, not knowing beforehand what he should do, trusted in the Lord and listened to the Spirit as he entered the city of Jerusalem. And, like Nephi, through the process of solving our problems and fulfilling our responsibilities, we will become more like God.

Chapter 5

OUR FEARS
DID CEASE

1 NEPHI 4:35–37

Today's world is a world of contracts and witnesses and end-less hours spent trying to void or circumvent or renegotiate some agreement. To many people, if an agreement is not in writing, it doesn't exist, and if it *is* in writing, there must be some way around it. Maybe this is why the following verses seem so amazing to us. Nephi and his brothers did not want the Jews to know about their family's journey into the wilderness, "lest they should pursue [them]" (1 Nephi 4:36). This meant that they had to prevent Laban's servant Zoram from telling the Jews where they were.

Nephi promised him that he would be a free man if he would go with them into the wilderness. Notice the amazing thing that took place when Zoram gave Nephi his answer: "And it came to pass that Zoram did take courage at the words which I spake. Now Zoram was the name of the servant; and he promised that he would go down into the wilderness unto our father. Yea, and he also made an oath unto us that he would tarry with us from that time forth. . . . And it came to pass that when Zoram had made an oath unto us, our fears did cease concerning him." (1 Nephi 4:35, 37.)

To these people there was nothing stronger or more sacred than a solemn oath. Most of them would give up their very lives before they would break an oath. Once Nephi and his brothers had received this oath from Zoram, they felt total confidence that he would not break his promise.

Jesus referred to these oaths six hundred years later as he sat on a hill overlooking the Sea of Galilee and gave the Sermon on the Mount. He said: "Again, ye have heard that it hath been said by them of old time, Thou shalt not forswear thyself [break your oath], but shalt perform unto the Lord thine oaths: but I say unto you, Swear not at all. . . . But let your communication be, Yea, yea; Nay, nay: for whatsoever is more than these cometh of evil." (Matthew 5:33–34, 37.)

Jesus replaced the law concerning oaths with a more perfect one and taught us that we do not need to swear an oath, or sign a contract, or have witnesses to some agreement. He expects us to just say yes or no and then keep our word.

It would be good for each of us to contemplate how well we follow this gospel law. Have we said that we would be a home teacher or a visiting teacher? If so, do we do our best to take care of the physical and spiritual needs of our families on a regular basis? If we commit ourselves to go to the temple, to help a neighbor, or to bring green Jell-O salad to the ward dinner, do we do everything we can do to keep that commitment? In the financial area of our lives, is our word more important to us than money or personal belongings?

The importance of our word is emphasized by a story told by President N. Eldon Tanner. He said that a young man once came to him and said that he had made an agreement with a man requiring him to make certain payments each month. He said that he was in arrears, and if he continued to make the payments, he would lose his house. He then asked President Tanner what he should do.

President Tanner told him to keep his agreement. The man was surprised and asked, "Even if it costs me my home?"

President Tanner replied, "I am not talking about your home. I am talking about your agreement; and I think your wife would rather have a husband who would keep his word, meet his obligations, keep his pledges or his covenants, and have to rent a home than to have a home with a husband who will not keep his covenants and his pledges." (*Improvement Era*, December 1966, p. 1137.)

One of the greatest things about God is that he is a God of truth who always keeps his word. If we are to become like him, we need to feel the same commitment to truth that he feels. As this commitment to truth permeates our lives, people will say of us, "They gave us their word, and our fears have ceased concerning them."

Chapter 6

MOST SWEET
ABOVE ALL

1 NEPHI 8, 11–12

The vision of the tree of life is one of the greatest visions ever received. It was received by both Lehi and Nephi. Many of the symbols found in this vision are discussed throughout the scriptures. The emphasis the vision places on the importance of the word of God is especially applicable in our day because of the widespread doctrine of the world that sin is good and that many of God's laws are foolish or outdated.

Some of the major symbols found in the vision of the tree of life are diagramed below. The interpretation of and an application for each symbol have been included. Scripture references are also given, so that you can read and mark these verses in your scriptures, if you so desire. All references are to 1 Nephi unless indicated otherwise. You may also desire to do some cross-referencing between the symbols and their interpretations.

Symbols	Interpretation	Application
Tree of life, Fruit of tree (8:10–12)	Love of God shown by the Savior's atonement, and eternal life (11:21–23; 15:36; D&C 14:7)	Partaking of the atonement of Christ brings true happiness and eventually leads to the celestial kingdom and to a fulness of joy.

Rod of iron (8:19)	Word of God (11:25; 15:23–24)	When we cling or hold fast to the word of God by listening to and obeying it, and press forward toward the celestial kingdom, Satan and his temptations have no power over us. (8:24; 15:24)
Great and spacious building (8:26–28)	Pride and wisdom of the world (11:35–36; 12:18)	When we get caught up in worldly knowledge and posessions, we become proud and lack the meekness and humility that are needed to receive and understand the word of God.
Mist of darkness (8:22–24)	Temptations of the devil (12:17)	If we do not have a firm hold on the word of God, the temptations that buffet us will blind us to the truth and harden us to the promptings of the Spirit. When this happens we wander onto broad roads and are lost. (12:17)
River of filthy water (8:13)	Depths or misery of hell (12:16; 15:26–29)	This filthy river represents the filthiness of sin. Those who have not repented and been cleansed of their sins are spiritually unclean. These people, who have let go of the iron rod and wandered into sin, are placed in spirit prison, or hell, where they suffer guilt and agony for their sins. (D&C 19:15–20)

The importance of understanding and implementing the principles taught in this vision was clearly demonstrated by a survey given to more than a hundred active Latter-day Saint teenagers.

They were asked how they decided what was right and what was wrong. The following answers are representative of most of the answers given:

1. "By how I felt about it."
2. "If I thought I would feel guilty, I wouldn't do it."
3. "If I thought I would feel happy, I would do it."
4. "I think of all the things that would happen if I did this or that; then I base my decision on that summary."
5. "If everything turns out OK, then I know I made the right decision."
6. "I don't know if it's right or wrong until I finish the task."
7. "I think to myself, If I choose this will I regret not choosing the other?"
8. "I look at how it will affect me."
9. "I try to think my decisions through to see what could happen."
10. "You can usually tell if it is right by the results of your choice."

At first glance, some of these answers may seem very good, but a little reflection reveals two important ingredients that have been left out of the decision-making process.

Lehi's vision represented this life and what we need to do in order to partake of eternal life and the happiness and joy that our Father has prepared for us. Those who tasted of the fruit of the tree were those who "did press forward through the mist of darkness, clinging to the rod of iron," that is, the word of God (1 Nephi 8:24). The idea of clinging to the word of God is an interesting one. Some synonyms of the word *clinging* are *adhering, cohering, sticking,* and *bonding.* Since not one of the teenagers mentioned studying the word of God or using the word of God in the decision-making process, it would be interesting to know how much clinging to the word is going on in their lives.

When we think about the great wisdom and knowledge of God, it seems foolish to even consider making decisions without using his word for guidance and direction. So many decisions are already made for us if we are studying and living the word of God. If we are offended, we don't need to decide whether to forgive the offender. If someone wants us to accept cash so that it won't affect our taxes, we don't have to waste our time wondering what to do.

If someone we are helping becomes pregnant out of wedlock, we don't have to wonder whether or not she should have an abortion. The Lord has already spoken on a vast range of topics such as family relationships, honesty, morality, dating, taking care of our yards, staying out of debt, working out disputes, and the type of entertainment we should seek. The first step in making any good decision might be to find out what the Lord has said on the subject.

Another important ingredient in clinging to the iron rod is to listen to the promptings of the Holy Ghost. The Holy Ghost can help us to apply gospel principles to specific areas and situations in our lives. However, this opportunity to have the Holy Ghost help us does not excuse us from studying the scriptures and other sources of the word of God. In fact, Elder Bruce R. McConkie suggested that we may be denied the guidance of the Holy Ghost if we make no effort to study the word of God:

> Our tendency—it is an almost universal practice among most Church members—is to get so involved with the operation of the institutional Church that we never gain faith like the ancients, simply because we do not involve ourselves in the basic gospel matters that were the center of their lives. . . .
>
> However talented men may be in administrative matters; however eloquent they may be in expressing their views; however learned they may be in worldly things—they will be denied the sweet whisperings of the Spirit that might have been theirs unless they pay the price of studying, pondering, and praying about the scriptures. (*Doctrines of the Restoration*, ed. Mark L. McConkie [Salt Lake City: Bookcraft, 1989], pp. 236, 238.)

As we study the vision of the tree of life, we might think of many different applications in our lives of its principles. Here are a few ideas:

1. As we partake of the fruit of the gospel through gospel living and accept the atonement of Jesus Christ, we can become truly happy (see 1 Nephi 8:10–12).

2. Once we feel the joy of the gospel, we desire to share it with others (see 1 Nephi 8:12). If we can help our children and those for whom we are responsible feel the joy of the gospel, they will desire to serve missions and share the gospel with others. This will have a

much greater effect than just telling them they should go on a mission.

3. The rod is made of iron, which is strong and firm and does not bend or break easily. I sometimes compare the iron rod to a railing that might be placed on the edge of a cliff to keep people from falling and destroying themselves on the rocks below. The iron rod extends along the river that represents the agony and depths of hell, and keeps us safe from this awful misery (see 1 Nephi 8:19).

4. Numberless concourses of people started on the path that led to the tree but *did not grab hold of the iron rod*. Because of temptation, all of them lost their way. (See 1 Nephi 8:21–23.)

5. In order to partake of the fruit we have to press forward and cling to the rod. Sometimes, because of temptations and problems that we face, we may have to cling with all the strength we possess, but the word of God will see us through. (See 1 Nephi 8:24.)

6. Some who had partaken of the fruit became ashamed and succumbed to social pressure and the acceptance of the world, and then they lost the great blessings that were theirs. We need to continue to grow and learn and endure to the end. (See 1 Nephi 8:25–28.)

7. Those who reached the tree of life held on to the iron rod continuously. Others felt their way towards the spacious building or drowned in the depths of hell. (See 1 Nephi 8:30–32.)

8. Nephi received the vision and came to understand its meaning as he was pondering the truths his father had taught him. We need to take time to ponder the word of God. (See 1 Nephi 11:1–6.)

9. The spacious building, which represents the pride of the world, fell—just as all those who accept the things of the world over the things of God will fall (see 1 Nephi 11:36).

10. Many times we do not lose our testimony or let go of the iron rod all at once. We just hold on to the word of God less and less firmly until it takes only a small breeze to break our hold. The scriptures refer to this process as *dwindling* in unbelief (see 1 Nephi 12:22).

Chapter 7

A BALL OF
CURIOUS WORKMANSHIP

1 NEPHI 16:28–29; ALMA 37:38–45

After the sons of Lehi returned to the wilderness with Ishmael's family, the sons and daughters of Lehi and Ishmael were married. The Lord then commanded Lehi to leave the next day and journey further into the wilderness. When Lehi awoke the next morning he found a round brass ball of "curious workmanship" outside his tent door. (In the Book of Mormon, *curious workmanship* means unusual or superior workmanship.) This ball had spindles, or pointers, that pointed the way they should travel, and writings would appear on it that taught them concerning the ways of the Lord. (See 1 Nephi 16:7–29.)

They named the ball *Liahona*, which, according to Alma, meant "compass" (Alma 37:38).

Nephi explained what made the pointers work: "They did work according to the faith and diligence and heed which we did give unto them. And there was also written upon them a new writing, which was plain to be read, which did give us understanding concerning the ways of the Lord; and it was written and changed from time to time, according to the faith and diligence which we gave unto it." (1 Nephi 16:28–29.)

More than five hundred years later, while preparing his son Helaman to become the steward of the sacred records, Alma referred to the Liahona. He pointed out that the Liahona had been prepared to show their fathers the course they should travel in the wilderness. He explained to Helaman that the Liahona had worked when faith and righteousness were exercised. He said that when their forefathers were slothful and forgot to exercise their faith and diligence, they did not progress in their journey but became lost and were afflicted with hunger and thirst. (See Alma 37:38–42.) Alma then made the following comparison:

> And now, my son, I would that ye should understand that these things are not without a shadow; for as our fathers were slothful to give heed to this compass (now these things were temporal) they did not prosper; even so it is with things which are spiritual.
>
> For behold, it is as easy to give heed to the word of Christ, which will point to you a straight course to eternal bliss, as it was for our fathers to give heed to this compass, which would point unto them a straight course to the promised land.
>
> And now I say, is there not a type in this thing? For just as surely as this director did bring our fathers, by following its course, to the promised land, shall the words of Christ, if we follow their course, carry us beyond this vale of sorrow into a far better land of promise. (Alma 37:43–45.)

Wouldn't it be exciting if an angel came to us and told us that we were going to have our own Liahona to guide us through this life's pitfalls so we could reach our promised land—the celestial kingdom? We would be able to look at this ball of curious workmanship, when faced with serious decisions, and it would point the way for us to go. During times of trial and confusion words would appear that would help us to better understand God's ways and our purposes here upon the earth.

According to Alma, each of us has the equivalent of the Liahona to guide us in our lives. We have not only the word of God but also the promise that the Holy Ghost will personally guide and direct us as we exercise our faith and diligently strive to keep God's commandments. When we are slothful we are left to ourselves to wander into paths that bring misery and heartache. When faithful, we are guided into decisions that bring peace and happiness.

All of us know that the Holy Ghost cannot dwell in an unclean tabernacle, yet sometimes we drift into paths that lead us away from the Holy Ghost and his promptings. Sometimes it takes a serious problem to make us analyze our direction and make adjustments in our course.

The purpose of the following quiz is to help us evaluate ourselves and determine whether we are doing the things that will allow the Holy Ghost to be operable in our lives. Answer the questions as if you were facing a serious problem or decision. If you really needed the help of the Holy Ghost during the next few days, what would your behavior be like as regards the following daily situations or activities? You may want to write your answers on a separate piece of paper.

1. What would your prayers be like?
2. What would your approach be to scripture study?
3. Would you feel comfortable with the current movies, videos, and TV programs that you watch? Which ones would you avoid?
4. Would you treat the members of your family the same way? If not, what changes would you make?
5. How would you feel about your worst enemy? Would you approach him to try to make things better?
6. Would you feel good about how you are spending your money, or would you do it differently?
7. How would you feel about the language you use? How would you change it?
8. What songs, musical groups, and stations would you listen to? Are there any that you listen to now that you would stop listening to?
9. Would you approach your Church assignment any differently? How about home or visiting teaching?
10. What about the time you spend with family or friends, at work, in Church service, or involved in entertainment? Would your time be divided any differently?

If we find that we would make some changes in our lives if we needed the help of the Holy Ghost, we may want to make those changes now anyway—because we do need the help of the Holy Ghost, daily. The wilderness in which Lehi and his family journeyed was not easy to navigate; likewise, the myriad paths and problems that the maze called earth life offers us hold many challenges. If Lehi needed the Liahona to reach his promised land, how much more do we need our personal Liahonas in order to reach the destination that we desire? Just as the Liahona was extremely sensitive to faith and righteousness, the Holy Ghost responds to our thoughts and actions today. How grateful we can be that the Lord has not left us alone but has given us this great gift. As we learn to fine tune our lives, the Holy Ghost will become an even more powerful and effective source of light and truth for us.

Chapter 8

AND HE
SUFFERETH IT

1 NEPHI 19:9

There may be many different reasons why we do things for others. We might do things out of a feeling of duty or because it is our responsibility. We might help someone because we know we should. We might do it because someone we respect asks us to. These reasons are probably good ones, but the best reasons for serving others are that we love them and we love God. The following scripture indicates that this was the main reason that Jesus suffered what he did for us: "And the world, because of their iniquity, shall judge him to be a thing of naught; wherefore they scourge him, and he suffereth it; and they smite him, and he suffereth it. Yea, they spit upon him, and he suffereth it, *because* of his loving kindness and his long-suffering towards the children of men." (1 Nephi 19:9, italics added.)

At one time we lived with our Heavenly Father and the Savior, and we felt their unconditional love for us. Because of the veil of forgetfulness that has fallen upon us in mortality, we come to rediscover and feel this love in new ways. As we accept the great gift of the Atonement and realize that we can be redeemed, this great feeling of love and appreciation expands within our souls.

Lehi explained his love for the Savior and the Savior's love for us in the following words: "But behold, the Lord hath redeemed my soul from hell; I have beheld his glory and I am encircled about eternally in the arms of his love" (2 Nephi 1:15). Another beautiful scriptural passage describing God's love appears in the book of Moses. Referring to Noah's ark, the record states that "the Lord smiled upon it, and held it in his own hand" (Moses 7:43). Each of us is buffeted with what seems to be a sea of sin, but these picturesque descriptions of God's love can help us realize that God will protect us and keep us safe from spiritual harm.

As we come to realize how much God and Jesus love us, we find ourselves desiring to return this love. Dolly Singleton is a good example of this. Dolly was a gray-haired grandmother whom the missionaries met while knocking on doors. As the missionaries taught her the first discussion, she took out a packet of tobacco and a piece of paper, and she proceeded to roll a cigarette by hand. She was so good at it that once the tobacco was in the paper she rolled the cigarette with one hand. This was both fascinating and depressing to the Elders.

By the time the first discussion was over Dolly had rolled and smoked three of these homemade cigarettes. She then made herself a cup of tea and offered a cup to each of the Elders, but of course they declined.

As Dolly continued to have the discussions and to roll and smoke her own cigarettes, the Elders began to dread the day they would teach the lesson about the Word of Wisdom. The day soon arrived, and as they set up their flannel board, Dolly started to smoke her first cigarette. The missionaries discussed the four things that members of the Church are asked to avoid and placed the word strips "tea," "coffee," "alcohol," and "tobacco" on the flannel board. Dolly continued to smoke throughout the discussion. When she was asked to identify the four things Heavenly Father did not want her to take into her body, she looked right through the smoke curling up from her cigarette and read the four words on the flannel board. When the Elders asked Dolly if she would commit herself to live the Word of Wisdom, she changed the subject and refused to make a commitment. The Elders asked her to pray about it and then left her—with a cigarette still in her hand.

The next day when the Elders returned to her home, Dolly shared the following story with them. She had decided the night before that the Word of Wisdom was too hard to live and had rolled three cigarettes and placed them on her mantel. She did this because she was too shaky in the morning to roll them. She then went to bed and tried to go to sleep, but every time she closed her eyes all she could see were the word strips on the flannel board—"tea," "coffee," "alcohol," and "tobacco," the substances Church members are to avoid.

Finally, at about two o'clock in the morning, she decided to kneel down and pray about the Word of Wisdom as the Elders had asked her to. As she asked Heavenly Father about the Word of Wisdom, she began to feel the great love that Heavenly Father had for her, and a scripture came into her mind: "God so loved the world, that he gave his only begotten Son" (John 3:16). Dolly started to cry as she realized how much God really loved her, and then she said to herself, *If God loves me this much and was willing to give up his Son for me, I can and will give up my cigarettes and tea for him.* Three weeks later she was a member of God's church here upon the earth.

Stories like Dolly's have taken place thousands of times. Jesus said that if we love him, we will keep his commandments (see John 14:15). If we reject the gift of the Atonement, we reject the Giver; but if we accept the gift, we become more like the Giver. The more we allow our hearts to be filled with love and our lives with service, the more we become like Jesus and our Father in Heaven. One of my favorite stories, whose source I can't recall, illustrates this well:

"One cold Christmas Eve day, a little boy of about six or seven was standing out in front of a store window. The little child had no shoes, and his clothes were mere rags. A young woman passing by saw the little boy and could read the longing in his pale blue eyes. She took the child by the hand and led him into the store. There she bought him some new shoes and a complete suit of warm clothing. They came back out into the street and the woman said to the child, 'Now, you go home and have a very merry Christmas.'

"The boy looked up at her and asked, 'Are you Jesus' mamma?'

"She smiled down at him and replied, 'No, son, I'm just one of his sisters.'

"The little boy then said, 'I knew you had to be some relation.'"

We are all related to God, which means that we are related, as well, to every person on this earth. As we reach out to others with love and kindness, not only do we become more like the Savior but we feel a greater kinship to our fellow brothers and sisters. We will notice that we also feel a closer affinity and nearness to God, who truly is our Father in Heaven.

Chapter 9

HE NUMBERETH
HIS SHEEP

1 NEPHI 22:25

Christ taught that he was the Good Shepherd. We can appreciate this even more when we realize how shepherds functioned at the time of Christ and how they still do in many parts of the world today. Some of us live in areas where there are sheepherders instead of shepherds. In my community, the sheep are driven by men on horseback and by dogs. They are forced and even scared into going a certain direction. Shepherds use a totally different approach.

Shepherds know each individual sheep and, many times, have a name for each one of them. Many shepherds take their small lambs and carry them in their arms until the lambs come to know and trust them. At the time of Christ the sheep were put in closed-in areas, called sheepfolds, at night. These areas had only one opening. Several different flocks of sheep could be placed in one sheepfold, and it took only one shepherd to watch over them. In the morning, when a shepherd came to get his sheep he would call them, and only his sheep would respond to his voice.

When a sheep is missing, most shepherds know which one it is. They know each sheep individually and are known by their sheep. Shepherds lead their sheep, and the sheep follow willingly. When I was in Israel I saw a flock of sheep grazing in a meadow. As I stopped to take a picture the shepherd said something to his sheep, turned his back to them, and started walking away. The sheep immediately began to line up in single file and to follow the shepherd. By this time I was clicking pictures at a tremendous rate.

By the time the shepherd had walked twenty yards, all of the sheep were following him. The shepherd then turned right and headed for the road where I was standing. When he reached the road, he turned left again and walked down the side of the road. The sheep, one by one, turned at the same place as the shepherd had, following him willingly. At about this time I ran out of film, but now I show the slides often to demonstrate the difference between a shepherd and a sheepherder.

The following quote shows the great interest that shepherds have for their sheep:

> As he is always with them, and so deeply interested in them, the shepherd comes to know his sheep very intimately. . . . At sunset the sheep are counted, usually two by two; but as a rule when they are brought together, the absence of any one is immediately *felt*. It is not only that one sheep is amissing, but the appearance of the whole flock seems to want something. This knowledge is so intimate and instinctively reliable that the formality of counting is often dispensed with. One day a missionary, meeting a shepherd on one of the wildest parts of the Lebanon, asked him various questions about his sheep, and among others if he counted them every night. On answering that he did not, he was asked how he knew if they were all there or not. His reply was, "Master, if you were to put a cloth over my eyes, and bring me any sheep and only let me put my hands on its face, I could tell in a moment if it was mine or not." Such is the fulness of meaning in the words of the Good Shepherd, "I know mine own, and mine own know me" (John 10:14). (George M. Mackie, *Bible Manners and Customs* [Fleming H. Revell Co., n.d.], p. 35.)

Jesus said: "I am the good shepherd: the good shepherd giveth his life for the sheep. . . . I am the good shepherd, and know my sheep, and am known of mine. . . . My sheep hear my voice, and I know them, and they follow me: and I give unto them eternal life; and they shall never perish, neither shall any man pluck them out of my hand." (John 10:11, 14, 27–28.)

While in Israel I also noticed the goats. When a shepherd spoke the sheep lined up and followed, but the goats continued to mill around the field and seemed to ignore the shepherd. In the scriptures those who do not follow the Savior and his teachings are referred to as goats. These people are described in the following verses of scripture: "O how marvelous are the works of the Lord, and how long doth he suffer with his people; yea, and how blind and impenetrable are the understandings of the children of men; for they will not seek wisdom, neither do they desire that she should rule over them. Yea, they are as a wild flock which fleeth from the shepherd, and scattereth, and are driven, and are devoured by the beasts of the forest." (Mosiah 8:20–21.)

When we understand the preceding ideas concerning sheep and shepherds, 1 Nephi 22:25 can become a great source of comfort and promise: "And he gathereth his children from the four quarters of the earth; and he numbereth his sheep, and they know him; and there shall be one fold and one shepherd; and he shall feed his sheep, and in him they shall find pasture."

If we will come to know Christ through obeying his word, he will feed us hope and love and give us great purpose and direction. To find pasture in the Savior is one of the greatest promises we could receive. It means that we will receive protection and peace and be nourished with the true bread of life. We will be filled instead of empty and feel safe instead of threatened. Our souls will be filled with peace instead of despair and discouragement, because we will know that the Savior is guiding and protecting us. He is giving us pasture.

The faith expressed by a woman who lived in France during World War I illustrates the promises of this scripture. Elder Hugh B. Brown and two other officers entered the city of Arras while it was under siege. The city had been evacuated, and Elder Brown thought that no one was in the city. He described what they found when they entered a cathedral:

> There we found a little woman kneeling at an altar. We paused, respecting her devotion. Then shortly she arose, wrapped her little shawl around her frail shoulders, and came tottering down the aisle. The man among us who could speak better French said, "Are you in trouble?"
>
> She straightened her shoulders, pulled in her chin, and said, "No, I'm not in trouble. I was in trouble when I came here, but I've left it there at the altar."
>
> "And what was your trouble?"

She said, "I received word this morning that my fifth son
has given his life for France. Their father went first, and then
one by one all of them have gone. But," straightening again, "I
have no trouble; I've left it there because I believe in the im-
mortality of the soul. I believe that men will live after death. I
know that I shall meet my loved ones again." (*Improvement Era*,
December 1969, p. 33.)

This faithful woman had received pasture from the Savior and
had fed on the nourishing truths that bring peace and comfort and
hope. These blessings are available to all of us as we respond to the
voice of the Good Shepherd and follow him.

Chapter 10

SATAN HAS
NO POWER

1 NEPHI 22:26

A few years ago a bishop was just leaving his office when the phone rang. He was in a hurry and didn't want to answer the phone, but he had a strong feeling that it was important. When he picked up the phone the voice on the other end said, "You don't know me and you will probably think this is some kind of joke, but I need help. Something evil is taking over my mind and I am scared. What can I do?"

The bishop learned that the caller was about ten minutes away and asked him to come to his office. While he was waiting for the man to arrive, the bishop knelt in humble prayer and asked for the Lord's help and guidance.

By this time the caller, whom we will refer to as Rick, had arrived. He was a young man, wild in appearance, and definitely in a state of panic. He told a frightening and tragic story that spanned the past several weeks of his life. Rick indicated that he was not a member of the Church but that he had been taught good Christian principles as a child. After he had left home he had departed from these principles and had violated most of what his parents had taught him.

For the past several weeks Rick had been feeling troubled, but this particular day at work he could actually feel some power gradually taking over his mind until he felt that just a small portion of his mind was still under his control. As he looked around his office he seemed to know the evil thoughts and desires of those he worked with. With the desperate realization that he was losing his identity to some outside power, he ran from the office where he worked.

Rick saw a phone booth and felt that his only chance was to talk to a man of God. He turned to the listing of churches in the yellow pages and started calling from the top of the list. After several unanswered calls he got through to a Relief Society sister, who gave him the bishop's number.

The bishop explained to Rick that he could receive a blessing that would solve the present crisis, but that a permanent solution lay in his hands alone, depending on whether he would correct his life to conform to the will of our Father in Heaven. The Spirit was strong as a blessing was given, and Rick immediately felt a feeling of peace and calm come over him.

The bishop discussed the gospel with Rick for several hours, and then Rick left for his home. The next morning the bishop contacted the stake missionaries in Rick's area and gave them Rick's phone number and address.

It was two or three weeks later when Rick called and invited the bishop to baptize him. His voice was enthusiastic, happy, and excited as he told how he had gained a personal testimony of the gospel.

Following Rick's baptism, he and the bishop sat alone in the dressing room and talked about the change that had taken place in his life. Tears streamed down their cheeks as they shared their testimonies with each other. Since that time Rick has served a mission and been sealed in the temple to a beautiful companion. He has a family of his own and has actively given his time in service to others.

Rick's experience is a perfect example of something that most of us already realize: There are two forces that can influence and guide our lives. When we fill our lives with thoughts and actions sponsored by Satan, we fall more and more under his influence. As we do the things the Lord wants us to do, we receive more guidance and direction from him.

Nephi writes about the Millennium and discusses what will restrict Satan's power during this thousand-year era. He says, "And because of the righteousness of [the Lord's] people, Satan has no power; wherefore, he cannot be loosed for the space of many years; for he hath no power over the hearts of the people, for they dwell in righteousness, and the Holy One of Israel reigneth" (1 Nephi 22:26).

The binding of Satan and his power will actually be "a result of two important actions by the Lord: (1) he will destroy telestial wickedness from the earth at his second coming; and (2) as a reward for heeding his counsels, the Lord will pour out his Spirit upon the righteous who remain to the extent that Satan's power will be overwhelmed. Thus, Satan will not have the power to tempt or negatively influence the Lord's people." (*Doctrine and Covenants Student Manual* [Salt Lake City: The Church of Jesus Christ of Latter-day Saints, 1981], p. 89.)

We do not have to wait until the Millennium to restrict the power and influence Satan wields in our lives. When Mormon was writing about Captain Moroni, he spent several verses talking about the great qualities that Moroni had. He then wrote, "Yea, verily, verily I say unto you, if all men had been, and were, and ever would be, like unto Moroni, behold, the very powers of hell would have been shaken forever; yea, the devil would never have power over the hearts of the children of men" (Alma 48:17).

With the help of the Lord, we can live in such a way as to limit the influence of Satan in our lives. It is important for us to evaluate the things that we invite into our lives, such as movies, books, magazines, and the TV shows we watch. Many of these things allow Satan to gain a greater foothold in our hearts and minds. The Lord wants us to resist Satan and to draw closer to the Spirit. He has promised us the power to overcome Satan and his influences. Jesus said, "Pray always, that you may come off conqueror; yea, that you may conquer Satan, and that you may escape the hands of the servants of Satan that do uphold his work" (D&C 10:5).

Chapter 11

FREE FOREVER
TO ACT FOR THEMSELVES

2 NEPHI 2:26–27

A few years ago a man named Charles wrote an article telling how his grandma had taught him to see. When Charles was six years old he had cut his foot on a broken bottle. His grandmother had bandaged it, but he had continued crying. His grandma put him on her knee and said, "Now, it'll be all right. Just think how lucky you are!" When Charles stopped crying and looked at her in surprise, she said, "If it had been your tongue cut in half you'd be in a purty pickle."

When Charles was twelve he was upset because it was raining and he wanted to play ball. He paced around the house until his grandma made him open the front door and sit down next to her. She then asked him several questions that he didn't want to answer because he didn't want to be happy about the rain. After pointing out that the "growing things can't go to the faucet and get a drink like you can," she asked him, "Would you want them to starve for a drink—just so's you can play ball?" When he refused to answer, she said, "Of course you wouldn't. And when it stops rainin', see how nice and clean the air will smell and how good it'll be to see the garden a-sproutin' and a-growin'. And all because you were unselfish enough not to play ball!"

As the years passed Charles's Grandma became almost totally blind. Once while Charles was on a trip, he purchased her an Indian blanket. He handed her the blanket and, without thinking, said, "It's an Indian blanket. I hope you like the color."

She felt its softness, then lifted it to her cheek and said, "I like the color, Charlie. It's the color of kindness—the color of love."

In retrospect, Charles wrote the following words about his grandmother: "Now, much later, I have a better understanding of what she tried to teach me through those years. She had shown me that eyes are merely the camera that takes the picture, and that it is the heart that develops it and colors it and decides whether the things we see are beautiful or drab, good or bad. . . . Though nearly blind herself, she had spared no effort to teach me how to see." (See Charles M. Manwaring, *Ensign*, August 1978, pp. 47–48.)

Charles's grandmother understood a great gospel principle and enriched the lives of those around her as she practiced it in her life. This great gospel truth was taught by Lehi to his son Jacob:

> And the Messiah cometh in the fulness of time, that he may redeem the children of men from the fall. And because that they are redeemed from the fall they have become free forever, knowing good from evil; to act for themselves and not to be acted upon, save it be by the punishment of the law at the great and last day, according to the commandments which God hath given.
>
> . . . And they are free to choose liberty and eternal life, through the great Mediator of all men, or to choose captivity and death, according to the captivity and power of the devil; for he seeketh that all men might be miserable like unto himself." (2 Nephi 2:26–27.)

According to Lehi, because of the Savior's atonement we are free to act for ourselves. But sometimes we react instead of act. We allow others or circumstances to decide how we feel and what we say or do. If we meet someone who is angry, we become angry. If someone yells at us, we yell back. We allow others to be the control center for our own feelings and even actions by reacting to them instead of acting for ourselves. As we do this we give up our freedom, and life's situations become the determining factor in how we feel and what we do.

Happiness is not found in our ability to control the things that happen around us. Happiness comes as we learn to control ourselves and live the gospel better. It comes as we quit reacting to negative stimuli around us and appreciate the great blessings the Lord has given us. It comes when, with the help of the Lord, we feel faith in God, hope for the future, and charity toward others. Satan wants us to be miserable, but God wants us to feel joy.

While Jesus was here on earth he set a perfect example of acting instead of reacting. He said and did what was right under all circumstances and conditions. We are not perfect yet, but as we decide to act for ourselves by facing obstacles and setbacks the way the Savior would, we will draw much closer to him. By making this a matter of sincere and frequent prayer, we can obtain the strength and understanding that we need from the Lord. To learn to act instead of react not only brings immediate happiness and satisfaction, as it did for Charles's grandmother, but it takes us a giant step closer to becoming like God and Jesus Christ.

Chapter 12

HE EMPLOYETH
NO SERVANT THERE

2 NEPHI 9:41

Many of us have been at an airport when a young man or woman has returned from a mission. When waiting family members see the plane taxi up to the unloading zone, they begin to crowd around the door. The airline representative usually has to tell them two or three times to back up a little bit so the passengers can unload. As the missionary is spotted, a cry of joy pierces the air, and the missionary is surrounded by excited friends and relatives. Kisses and hugs are shared as love for one another is expressed.

As exciting and joyful and emotional as a missionary homecoming is, it cannot match the great reunion we will have with God and Jesus as we gain our exaltation. As the following scripture says, Jesus will meet us personally: "O then, my beloved brethren, come unto the Lord, the Holy One. Remember that his paths are righteous. Behold, the way for man is narrow, but it lieth in a straight course before him, and the keeper of the gate is the Holy One of Israel; and he employeth no servant there; and there is none other way save it be by the gate; for he cannot be deceived, for the Lord God is his name." (2 Nephi 9:41.)

This one verse of scripture contains much that we can ponder and apply in our lives. Think about the coming reunion that we will have with Jesus as we examine some of the phrases found in this important verse.

Come unto the Lord, the Holy One. If we are going to have a joyful reunion, we need to follow the path that leads to the Lord and to our Father in Heaven. Jacob says that his paths are righteous, and he describes the path that leads us back to God.

Behold, the way for man is narrow, but it lieth in a straight course before him. All through the scriptures the path is called the strait and narrow way. Sin puts us on detours and side roads and forbidden paths that lead to destruction and unhappiness. The strait and narrow path leads to exaltation and a fulness of joy. Notice that the path "lieth in a straight course" before us. The path may be narrow, but there are no deceptive curves or secret drop-offs that have been placed to fool us. The Lord has shown us the way, and it is clearly marked before us. He has given us his word (the iron rod) so that we will have something to cling to. He has even promised us that he will help us to overcome any obstacle or roadblock that we encounter as we travel along the path.

Now comes the heart of the scripture: *The keeper of the gate is the Holy One of Israel; and he employeth no servant there.* Elder Neal A. Maxwell explained his feelings about this great reunion and why the Savior will be there personally to greet us. He quoted this verse and then referred to Mormon 6:17, which indicates that Jesus stands with open arms to receive us. Elder Maxwell then said: "That's why he's there! He waits for you 'with open arms.' That imagery is too powerful to brush aside. . . . It is imagery that should work itself into the very center core of one's mind—a rendezvous impending, a moment in time and space, the likes of which there is none other. And that rendezvous is a reality. I certify that to you. He does wait for us with open arms, because his love of us is perfect." (*But a Few Days*, address to religious educators [Salt Lake City: The Church of Jesus Christ of Latter-day Saints, 1983], p. 7.)

Just as loved ones want to be present when missionaries return, the Savior wants to be present when we return to him. Just as "Alma did rejoice exceedingly to see his brethren" and felt even more joy because "they were still his brethren in the Lord" (Alma 17:2), the Savior will rejoice with us as we return to live with him again. As Elder Maxwell said, this reunion will be like no other.

Chapter 13

NOT HANG
DOWN OUR HEADS

2 NEPHI 10:20, 23

Truman Madsen pointed out the significance of a vision that Joseph Smith had:

> The Prophet [Joseph Smith] saw in panoramic vision at least nine of the Twelve in a foreign land. (He doesn't say England, but that is where they eventually went.) He saw them gathered in a circle, without shoes, beaten, tattered, discouraged. Standing above them in the air was the Lord Jesus Christ. And it was made known to the Prophet that He yearned to show Himself to them, to reach down and lift them. But they did not see Him. The Savior looked upon them and wept. We are told by two of the brethren who heard Joseph rehearse that vision that he could never speak of it without weeping himself. Why? Why should he be so touched? Because Christ willingly came to the earth so that all of the Father's family could come to him boldly, knowing that he knows what is taking place in us when we sin, that he knows all our feelings and cares. The greatest tragedy of life is that having paid that awful price of suffering "according to the flesh that his bowels might be filled with compassion" and now prepared to reach down and help us, he is forbidden because we won't let him. We look down instead of up. (*Ensign*, January 1976, p. 23.)

When we look down instead of up, we forget the great blessings that God has given us, which include the Atonement and the chance to repent. God does not want us to feel worthless; he wants us to feel repentant. Jacob taught the people of Nephi this same principle when he said, "And now, my beloved brethren, seeing that our merciful God has given us so great knowledge concerning these things, let us remember him, and lay aside our sins, and not hang down our heads, for we are not cast off. . . . Therefore, cheer up your hearts, and remember that ye are free to act for yourselves—to choose the way of everlasting death or the way of eternal life." (2 Nephi 10:20, 23.)

The word *Gospel* means "good news." The good news is that Jesus, through his atonement, has made it possible for us to return to our Father in Heaven. As we gain testimonies of the gospel, this good news should fill our hearts with joy.

When Lehi partook of the fruit of the tree—the tree representing the love of God as expressed through the atonement of Christ—he said that it "filled my soul with exceedingly great joy; wherefore, I began to be desirous that my family should partake of it also; for I knew that it was desirable above all other fruit" (1 Nephi 8:12).

As the good news fills our hearts with joy, we also have the desire to share the gospel with others. Our Church callings become enjoyable as we keep this goal in mind. Sometimes we get so caught up in meetings and programs and structure that we forget the simpleness of the gospel and of the Lord's message. Jesus told us that we should "say nothing but repentance unto this generation" (D&C 6:9). He also said, "How great is his [Jesus'] joy in the soul that repenteth!" (D&C 18:13.) The "marvelous work and a wonder" talked about in the scriptures (see Isaiah 29:14) can be thought of as referring to the marvelous and wonderful changes that take place in people's lives as they accept the atonement of Christ and receive direction and purpose and joy in their lives. This marvelous work is the very center and purpose of all Church service. Every lesson taught should be directed toward helping people turn more toward God and Jesus. Everything a leader does should be directed toward bringing people to Christ. When this is the center and purpose of our service, joy is a natural by-product.

One sister, who had lost sight of the purpose of the gospel and of the Church, had an experience that helped her recatch the vision. Joan had held many important positions in the Church but had become "weary in well-doing," and her Church assignments had become a burden to her. She played tennis with a group of ladies, one of whom was not a member of the Church. This non-member was always happy and cheerful, and she seemed to get a great deal of joy out of life.

One day Joan asked her friend why she was so happy. The nonmember then told her it was because of the service she per-formed in her church. She related how she spent many hours each week helping people and how the Lord had blessed her. As Joan listened, she realized that the situation should have been reversed. *She* should have been telling her nonmember friend why *she* was so happy. She perceived that she had allowed her Church service to become a burden rather than an opportunity to help others come closer to God. As Joan made some adjustments in her life, she began to again feel the joy that comes from spreading the "good news."

God wants us to be happy, and he has shared many reasons with us why we should be happy. Jesus said, "Be of good cheer; thy sins be forgiven thee" (Matthew 9:2). Just before he was crucified, Jesus told his Apostles to "be of good cheer; I have overcome the world" (John 16:33). In the latter days the Savior said that we should "be of good cheer, and . . . not fear, for I the Lord am with you, and will stand by you" (D&C 68:6). After several elders had faced many dangers, the Lord told them, "What I say unto one I say unto all, be of good cheer, little children; for I am in your midst, and I have not forsaken you" (D&C 61:36). God wants us to be happy both here and in the eternities. He doesn't want us to feel sorry for ourselves and walk around looking at the ground. He de-sires that we look to him, take advantage of the Atonement, and share the good news with others. In a revelation given through Joseph Smith, the Lord said: "Ye have not as yet understood how great blessings the Father hath in his own hands and prepared for you; and ye cannot bear all things now; nevertheless, be of good cheer, for I will lead you along. The kingdom is yours and the bless-ings thereof are yours, and the riches of eternity are yours." (D&C 78:17–18.)

Chapter 14

WE REJOICE
IN CHRIST

2 NEPHI 25:23, 26

Many members of the Church wonder why other Christian religions do not accept us as Christians even though the Church is named after the Savior and we teach about Jesus. One of the basic reasons for this may be partly our own fault. Much of the Christian world teaches that we are saved by grace, not by anything we do. When members of The Church of Jesus Christ of Latter-day Saints are asked if they believe in salvation by grace, many respond that they do not. They say that we are saved through our obedience and through our works. This, of course, is not correct.

The very core of our doctrine is the atonement of Jesus Christ, yet some may underestimate the importance of the Atonement and our helplessness without it. A few years ago *Newsweek* magazine wrote an article about the Church. This article did not deal with the doctrine of the Church but supposedly reported what some Latter-day Saints actually believed. This article stated: "Unlike orthodox Christians, Mormons believe that men are born free of sin and earn their way to godhood by the proper exercise of free will, rather than through the grace of Jesus Christ. Thus Jesus' suffering and death in the Mormon view . . . do not atone for the sins of others." (*Newsweek*, 1 September 1980, p. 68.)

I'm sure that most of us have a deeper understanding of the Atonement and where we would be without the grace of Christ than this article indicated. There is no way that any of us can return to our Father in Heaven, no matter how righteous we are, without his grace and mercy. One of the best statements concerning the Atonement was given by Nephi when he wrote, "For we labor diligently to write, to persuade our children, and also our brethren, to believe in Christ, and to be reconciled to God; for we know that *it is by grace that we are saved, after all we can do.* . . . And we talk of Christ, we rejoice in Christ, we preach of Christ, we prophesy of Christ, and we write according to our prophecies, that our children may know *to what source they may look* for a remission of their sins." (2 Nephi 25:23, 26, italics added.)

I have heard these verses discussed many times. Most of the time the emphasis has been on the part that says "after all we can do." Maybe we need to emphasize more the fact that, after all we can do, it is by "grace that we are saved."

As one stake president sat in his ward's fast and testimony meeting, he noticed that not one person had mentioned Jesus or the Atonement other than by closing talks or prayers in the name of Jesus. Nephi said, "We talk of Christ, we rejoice in Christ, [and] we preach of Christ," but none of that took place during this particular meeting. The stake president wondered whether this was an exception to the rule or if there was a problem in his stake. He asked the members of the high council to monitor their wards during the next fast and testimony meetings and see how many people actually thanked the Savior for his atonement or referred to this great blessing in some way. He was shocked to find that, in the eight wards, only three people had mentioned their gratitude for the Atonement or discussed the Savior in any way. Although it is true that we should feel grateful for our families and for the bishop and for those who have helped us during the past month, we should realize that the greatest and most important service that has ever been offered us is the atonement of Jesus Christ. Somehow, naturally, because of our gratitude and love for the Savior, it should be uppermost in our hearts and minds.

Jacob said that without the Atonement we would become "angels to a devil, to be shut out from the presence of our God, and to remain with the father of lies, in misery, like unto himself." He went onto say, "O how great the goodness of our God, who prepareth a way for our escape from the grasp of this awful monster; yea, that monster, death and hell." (2 Nephi 9:9–10.)

President Thomas S. Monson described the debt we owe Jesus

when he said, "We laugh, we cry, we work, we play, we love, we live. And then we die. And dead we would remain but for one man and his mission, even Jesus of Nazareth." (*Ensign*, April 1990, p. 5.)

The Savior did not just suffer for our sins and then distance himself from us. He is constantly there to bless us with comfort, guidance, and strength. He desires to bless every part of our lives. The following words of one of our sacrament hymns portray well the role of the Savior and beautifully describe how most of us feel about him. As we read these words, it may be helpful for us to ponder what we and our families can do to better remember and appreciate the Savior and his atonement.

> I know that my Redeemer lives.
> What comfort this sweet sentence gives!
> He lives, he lives, who once was dead.
> He lives, my ever-living Head.
> He lives to bless me with his love.
> He lives to plead for me above.
> He lives my hungry soul to feed.
> He lives to bless in time of need.
>
> He lives to grant me rich supply.
> He lives to guide me with his eye.
> He lives to comfort me when faint.
> He lives to hear my soul's complaint.
> He lives to silence all my fears.
> He lives to wipe away my tears.
> He lives to calm my troubled heart.
> He lives all blessings to impart.
>
> He lives, my kind, wise heav'nly Friend.
> He lives and loves me to the end.
> He lives, and while he lives, I'll sing.
> He lives, my Prophet, Priest, and King.
> He lives and grants me daily breath.
> He lives, and I shall conquer death.
> He lives my mansion to prepare.
> He lives to bring me safely there.

He lives! All glory to his name!
He lives, my Savior, still the same.
Oh, sweet the joy this sentence gives:
"I know that my Redeemer lives!"

("I Know That My Redeemer Lives,"
Hymns, no. 136.)

Chapter 15

WHO SEETH US?

2 NEPHI 27:27

Phil and his family had just moved into a small community when he was called to be the Scoutmaster. Since he didn't have time to plan an activity for the first night, he decided to take the boys on a night hike. Phil had seen a winding dirt road just outside of town. Next to the road was a little brook, and the road was lined with beautiful trees whose branches swept out over the road. It was one of the prettiest spots Phil had ever seen. He chose this area for his night hike, not realizing that it was where some of the teenagers from the town went to "park."

As the Scouts were hiking they spotted a car parked fifty yards up the road. Before their new Scoutmaster could stop them they took off at high speed for the car. Inside the car was a couple who had deliberately chosen a dark, secluded spot so they would not be seen. When the Scouts reached the car they surrounded it and pressed their faces up against the windows so they could look inside. The couple, who thought they were completely alone and would not be disturbed, were shocked when they looked up and saw the myriad faces staring through the windows.

At about this time the Scoutmaster arrived, and after taking one glance through the window, he hurried the boys away from the car, nearly panic-stricken. This was the last night hike the troop took for many months.

This couple had a misunderstanding that seems to be shared by many others. They thought that by finding a dark, secluded spot they could sin and not be caught. They failed to take into account that none of us can ever be alone. Besides the Scouts watching through the windows, there were many others who knew what this couple was doing. The two may have looked all around themselves, but they failed to look up. God, Jesus, and the Holy Ghost were aware of what was going on. Many loved ones on the other side of the veil who care about them may also have been aware of their actions. Certainly some of the spirits that followed Satan were present and rejoicing. Actually, a whole group of witnesses was there long before the Scouts arrived.

The next time we find ourselves thinking we can sin and no one will know about it, it may help to think about a warning that President Spencer W. Kimball gave. He said: "There are dark corners and hidden spots and closed cars in which . . . transgression can be committed, but to totally conceal it is impossible. There is no night so dark, no room so tightly locked, no canyon so closed in, no desert so totally uninhabited that one can find a place to hide from his sins, from himself, or from the Lord. Eventually, one must face the great Maker." (*The Teachings of Spencer W. Kimball*, ed. Edward L. Kimball [Salt Lake City: Bookcraft, 1982], p. 266.)

Nephi saw our day and prophesied many things about it. He must have seen this mistaken idea that by seeking the dark we can sin and get away with it, for he said, "And wo unto them that seek deep to hide their counsel from the Lord! And their works are in the dark; and they say: who seeth us, and who knoweth us?" (2 Nephi 27:27.)

When we find ourselves looking furtively around or looking for dark or secluded places before we do something, chances are we are doing something that Satan wants us to do, for Satan is the founder of "works of darkness"—but God "worketh not in darkness" (see 2 Nephi 26:22–23). Since God works not in darkness, neither should we. When we do things that bring us peace and satisfaction instead of embarrassment and turmoil, we please not only ourselves but also God and those around us as well—for the things of God really do bring contentment and fulfillment.

Chapter 16

CAREFULLY DOWN TO HELL

2 NEPHI 28:21–25

A few years ago a man decided to walk from California to New York. When he reached the halfway point reporters interviewed him. By then he had walked over fifteen hundred miles, and they wondered what his greatest obstacle had been. They expected it had been the tall mountain passes, the hot dry stretches of desert, or the weather—the sun, the wind, or the rain. They were surprised when he said that his greatest problem was the sand that kept getting in his shoes.

If this sand was not taken care of immediately, it would soon cause blisters on his feet and eventually stop his cross-country walk completely. Something as small as a grain of sand could lead to defeat.

There is an important correlation between this man's physical progress and our spiritual progress. Satan knows that we have set high standards and expectations for ourselves. He would like us to be immoral or grossly dishonest or violent toward our family and others. But he can't get us to bite at these things because they are just too big. Instead, he gets us to nibble at something that will eventually lead to these bigger sins. These "small" sins become spiritual grains of sand in our lives. They lead to increasingly bigger problems until our spiritual progression is completely stopped.

Satan's plan is to introduce spiritual grains of sand into our lives without our even being aware of them. Small sins lead to larger and larger sins until, before we know it, our lives are full of boulders. Nephi warned us of this common approach used by Satan:

> And others will he pacify, and lull them away into carnal security, that they will say: All is well in Zion; yea, Zion prospereth, all is well—and thus the devil cheateth their souls, and leadeth them away carefully down to hell.
>
> And behold, others he flattereth away, and telleth them there is no hell; and he saith unto them: I am no devil, for there is none—and thus he whispereth in their ears, until he grasps them with his awful chains, from whence there is no deliverance. . . .
>
> Therefore, wo be unto him that is at ease in Zion!
>
> Wo be unto him that crieth: All is well! (2 Nephi 28:21–22, 24–25.)

Nephi described how Satan leads us: "The devil . . . is the founder of all these things; yea, the founder of murder, and works of darkness; yea, and he leadeth them by the neck with a flaxen cord, until he bindeth them with his strong cords forever" (2 Nephi 26:22).

Flax is a blue-flowered plant that is grown for its fiber. These small fibers are used for making linen. Satan introduces us to very small sins, like fine flaxen fibers, and because we are not on our guard, we invite these sins into our lives. These small sins open our lives to increasingly larger sins until the fine flaxen fibers become "strong cords" and "awful chains" and we have been led "carefully down to hell."

A small community was once faced with real disaster. A teenager was having a bad day, and in anger and frustration he left his home and went for a drive. As he drove past the high school he saw the dumpster in the back parking lot. His family had owned the trash contract for the school district but had recently lost it to a competitor. Because of his feelings of anger and resentment, he decided to start a fire in the dumpster. This young man was not a bad person but was just overreacting to his negative feelings. These negative feelings can be compared to grains of sand causing irritation in his life.

The fire grew more quickly than he had thought it would and soon spread to the roof of the high school. Before the night was over the high school burned to the ground. Millions of dollars' worth of damage was done. Hundreds of students lost all of their personal belongings. The teachers lost all of the equipment and files that they had been building for years.

The high school students had to go to school at the middle school during the afternoons and evenings for two or three years until the high school was rebuilt. The effect on the boy and on his family was catastrophic. Thousands of lives were affected from this one small act.

This is the way sin works in our lives. It starts as a small spark but quickly fans into flames and eventually devours our whole lives if we are not careful. Satan "carefully" gets others to repeat this same pattern over and over again.

One young couple shared with their bishop the chain of events that had led to the loss of their chastity. It had all started with the telling of an off-color joke. The joke was not all that bad, but other jokes followed until the Spirit was gone and the mood for necking and petting had taken its place. This necking and petting eventually led to a complete loss of chastity and virtue. This couple were convinced that without the first off-color joke they would have still been morally clean.

The Savior also discussed the importance of keeping small sins out of our lives: "And if thy right eye offend thee [cause thee to stumble], pluck it out, and cast it from thee. . . . And if thy right hand offend thee, cut it off, and cast it from thee: for it is profitable for thee that one of thy members should perish, and not that thy whole body should be cast into hell." (Matthew 5:29–30.)

A sixteen-year-old boy named Mack was working on his farm when his right hand and left foot got caught in a corn picker. In order to save his life, he pulled and kicked until he literally tore his right arm and left foot off.

Mack somehow crawled back onto the corn picker and drove it to his house. He then got into his family's pickup truck and drove himself eight miles to the hospital. The strength and courage that Mack demonstrated in order to save his life is astonishing. If we are to save our spiritual lives, we have to be as committed as Mack was, in getting rid of the sins that are pulling us down.

After quoting 2 Nephi 28:21, Elder George Albert Smith said, "Now, I want you to note that: 'And thus the devil cheateth their souls and leadeth them away carefully down to hell.' And that is the way he does it, that's exactly the way he does it. He does not come and grab you bodily and take you into his territory, but he whispers, 'Do this little evil,' and when he succeeds in that, another little evil and another, and, to use the expression quoted, 'He cheateth their souls.' That's what he does. He makes you believe that you are gaining something when you are losing." (In Conference Report, April 1918, p. 40.)

As we empty the sands of sin out of our lives and jerk ourselves free from the sins that are pulling us down, we will feel the great freedom that comes from obedience and from being liberated from Satan's flaxen cords. We will also notice the increased influence and guidance that will come to us from the Holy Ghost.

Chapter 17

HEALETH
THE WOUNDED SOUL

JACOB 2:8

More than thirty American soldiers were captured and placed in an enemy prison camp. They were beaten with clubs, kicked, had guns placed to their heads, and were told that if they didn't give the information that was asked for, they would be killed. This type of cruel treatment went on day after day and week after week. During these desperate months of torture and interrogation the soldiers received the strength they needed from prayer and from the scriptures.

At first, the prisoners tried to give thanks at meals, but the guards beat them every time they were seen praying. When they began to pray silently, if the guards noticed their lips moving, they were still beaten. These beatings actually sparked the desire to pray even more.

Anytime two or more of the prisoners were together without a guard to hear, they helped each other recall passages of scripture from the Bible. Their favorite scripture became the twenty-third Psalm, which they slowly pieced together: "Yea, though I walk through the valley of the shadow of death, I will fear no evil: for thou art with me; thy rod and thy staff they comfort me."

They wrote the scriptures they could remember on bits and scraps of paper which became known as their prisoner's Bible. When they returned home, they testified of the great strength they had received from the scriptures. Especially comforting to them were the Old Testament stories that described how God had helped deliver his followers from bondage and oppression.

There are so many different blessings that can come to us from scripture study. These prisoners received one of the greatest of all blessings—peace and comfort to their souls. Most of us aren't prisoners in a camp or in a stockade, but all of us, from time to time, are filled with fear, anxiety, and conflict. We face such problems as death, serious sickness, conflict at home and work, emotional and physical abuse, guilt and fear caused by sin, and many other soul-churning problems.

Jacob explained in a most beautiful and inspiring way the great effect the word of God can have on our troubled souls: "And it supposeth me that they have come up hither to hear the pleasing word of God, yea, the word which healeth the wounded soul" (Jacob 2:8).

All of us can receive this healing power from the scriptures as we strive to live the gospel and make scripture study an important part of our lives. The following story depicts the great power of the scriptures to "heal the wounded soul."

A young man named Richard was filled with resentment and rebellion against his family and the Church. He left home and joined the military. He became so deeply involved in sin and so depressed that he eventually ended up confined to a padded cell in a mental hospital.

While there he remembered that his father had once said, "Richard, when you hit rock bottom, turn to the scriptures." He decided to read the Book of Mormon just to show that his father was wrong, but in spite of his negative attitude, something good began to happen to him. By the time he had read the Book of Mormon seven times, he had received a testimony and the desire and strength to straighten out his life. With each reading, hope, peace, and love poured into his wounded soul. It wasn't many years before Richard knelt across a temple altar from a beautiful young woman and sincerely made eternal covenants with God. (From James M. Paramore, in the *Hold to the Rod* series, Scripture Motivation lesson outline, lesson 4, p. 9.)

The word of God healed Richard's wounded soul just as it will heal each of us as we allow the great truths of the scriptures to sink deep into our hearts. To feast upon the words of God is to study his word and make it part of our lives. A Thanksgiving feast wouldn't be all that enjoyable if we just sat around the table and sniffed the different aromas that accompany such a meal. To receive strength and enjoyment from the meal, we partake of it and digest it and make it a part of us. So it is with the scriptures. To just sit in the same room with them or taste them or even snack from them is not enough. The healing power of God comes into our souls when we partake of the scriptures by studying them and then applying them so that their truths become an integral part of us.

Chapter 18

YE SHALL OBTAIN RICHES

JACOB 2:17–19

Shortly after the wife of Elder L. Tom Perry passed away, he gave an inspiring talk about her in conference. In this talk he shared the great love for others that his wife had demonstrated in so many different ways. Elder Perry shared the following example of her generosity:

> As a family we soon learned to live with the unexpected when an act of charity was involved. We had moved to California several years ago, and while we were preparing our finances to buy a home, we rented one which furnished us with appliances we needed. We had to store ours in our garage waiting for the purchase of a home. One evening in sacrament meeting she heard an earnest appeal from the bishop of our ward to assist those who had lost so much in a devastating flood a few miles from where we lived. As I drove home from work a few nights later, I saw a trailer in my driveway. There was a man tying my appliances on his trailer. I rushed into the house to see what was going on. And I was greeted with the words, "Oh, didn't I tell you? After sacrament meeting last week, I informed the bishop if anyone needed our appliances for flood relief, they could have them." (*Ensign*, May 1975, p. 32.)

Sister Perry's attitude toward her appliances is an inspiring example of what Jacob taught his people concerning riches and worldly possessions. He said: "Think of your brethren like unto yourselves, and be familiar with all and free with your substance, that they may be rich like unto you. But before ye seek for riches, seek ye for the kingdom of God. And after ye have obtained a hope in Christ ye shall obtain riches, if ye seek them; and ye will seek them for the intent to do good—to clothe the naked, and to feed the hungry, and to liberate the captive, and administer relief to the sick and the afflicted." (Jacob 2:17–19.)

There is nothing wrong with having—or even seeking— worldly possessions if our attitude is right. President Gordon B. Hinckley said:

> No matter our financial circumstances, we want to improve them. This, too, is good if it is not carried to an extreme. I am satisfied that the Father of us all does not wish His children to walk in poverty. He wants them to have comforts and some of the good things of the earth. In the Old Testament, He speaks of "a land flowing with milk and honey," of the fatlings of the flock, and of other things which indicate that He would have His children properly fed and clothed and sheltered, enjoying the comforts that come of the earth, but not to excess.
>
> It is when greed takes over, when we covet that which others have, that our affliction begins. And it can be a very sore and painful affliction. (*Ensign,* March 1990, p. 4.)

The problem with riches is that they can quickly become our god. Nephi identified this problem when he warned: "But wo unto the rich, who are rich as to the things of the world. For because they are rich they despise the poor, and they persecute the meek, and their hearts are upon their treasures; wherefore, their treasure is their god. And behold, their treasure shall perish with them also." (2 Nephi 9:30.)

Jacob counseled that we should seek first the kingdom of God and then worry about the riches of the world. He indicated that when we put these two things in the proper order we will use the physical possessions we are blessed with to bless the lives of others. That does not mean that we need to become wealthy before we can share what we have. Jacob said that we may obtain riches, but he never promised that we would be rich. All of us have many opportunities to help those in need. Elder Marvin J. Ashton taught: "The main question for every person to resolve is not what he would do if he had vast money, time, influence, or educational advantages, but how he will best use the means and assets he has and will yet have. . . . One of life's great lessons is to teach us that what we do with what we have is more important than what we have." (*Ensign*, September 1982, pp. 72, 75.)

One family, even with two missionaries in the field, still contributes to other families that are supporting missionaries. It would be easy for them to feel that supporting two missionaries of their own fulfills their missionary obligation, but this is not the case. It is not that they are rich, but as they compare their financial condition with that of other families, they feel a need to help. Their burden of supporting two missionaries is not so great as the financial burden some families face when supporting only one missionary. Riches and wealth are relative. All of us are both richer and poorer than someone around us.

The key to living this principle—and all other principles of the gospel—is simply one of priorities. When we put the Lord first in our lives, other areas of our lives seem to improve. President Ezra Taft Benson promised us: "When we put God first, all other things fall into their proper place or drop out of our lives. Our love of the Lord will govern the claims for our affection, the demands on our time, the interests we pursue, and the order of our priorities." (*Ensign*, May 1988, p. 4.)

Chapter 19

DELIGHT IN CHASTITY

JACOB 2:28

After teaching the law of chastity to his students, a seminary teacher asked them to respond to the question, Why stay morally clean? The following response was typical of the many good answers that were given: "The very key of the plan of happiness is to create, within the bonds of marriage, a body for a heavenly soul. Sex is good and sacred when it is used to express true love between marriage partners, and not when it is used just for lust. The Lord has given us guidelines so that we can protect ourselves and not misuse this power."

The young woman who gave this answer has come to understand that, in our quest for exaltation, there are few things more important than how we use the God-given power to have children. This power of procreation is the very core of our Heavenly Father's plan. Because of the significance of this eternal power, it is important for all of us to evaluate our thoughts, desires, and behavior in this area. It is not a topic that should be reserved for teenagers only.

The gap between what the world teaches and what God teaches is growing wider each day. God teaches that the power of creation is sacred and should be used only within the bonds of marriage. Even then we are to use wisdom and restraint. On the other hand, the world teaches that this power of creation is only a physical appetite to be satisfied along with all of our other appetites. Television, films, jokes, literature, advertisements, and everyday conversation all work together to degrade and cheapen this special power. Because Satan knows how important this power is, he works overtime trying to persuade us to misuse it.

Elder Boyd K. Packer warned us of Satan and his plan:

> In the beginning there was one among us who rebelled at the plan of our Heavenly Father. He vowed to destroy and to disrupt the plan.
>
> He was prevented from having a mortal body and was cast out—limited forever from establishing a kingdom of his own. He became satanically jealous. He knows that this power of creation is not just an incident to the plan, but a key to it.
>
> He knows that if he can entice you to use this power prematurely, to use it too soon, or to misuse it in any way, you may well lose your opportunities for eternal progression.
>
> He is an actual being from the unseen world. He has great power. He will use it to persuade you to transgress those laws set up to protect the sacred powers of creation. (*Ensign*, July 1972, p. 112.)

The first step in staying morally clean is to understand just how important the law of chastity is. Jacob didn't leave much room for doubt when he gave his people the word of the Lord: "For I, the Lord God, delight in the chastity of women. And whoredoms are an abomination before me; thus saith the Lord of Hosts." (Jacob 2:28.)

God wants us to use this power correctly because some of the greatest blessings come from respecting the sanctity of life and living the law of chastity. When a couple participates in the sacred act of procreation, they become partners with God in the creation of a human life. It is almost overwhelming to realize that a spirit child of God is placed into a physical body that we create, and a living soul is born. Through this sacred physical union, we actually introduce divine individuals into their second estate.

Once we realize the sacredness of sexual intimacy, we need to ensure that it remains sacred to us. Our feelings concerning this power can be eroded so subtly and so quickly that we may not even realize it is happening. We may find ourselves chuckling at off-color stories or watching TV shows and videos that would have appalled us several years ago.

Now is a good time to evaluate every activity in our lives to see if we are allowing the world's view of sex to infiltrate our thoughts or actions in any way. Once we have done this, studying the word of God and praying for the power to resist temptation can give us the spiritual strength we need to withstand or eliminate activities that cheapen and erode this special power.

Chapter 20

SUNK DEEP
INTO MY HEART

ENOS 1:1–16

Sometimes we get discouraged because we sense that our children are not feeling as deeply committed to the gospel as we would like. They participate in Church activities and seem to live all of the "big" commandments, but they argue with each other, demonstrate streaks of selfishness, and sometimes seem insensitive to the feelings of others. These and other weaknesses cause us to worry that our children aren't developing the strong personal testimony that they need in order to successfully live the gospel in this challenging world. Sometimes all that is missing is time and experience.

Such may have been the case with Enos, who was the son of Jacob. When Jacob was about to die he gave the plates to Enos. He told Enos the things he had been commanded to do by Nephi, and Enos promised he would do these things. Jacob then bid farewell to those who would read the plates. (See Jacob 7:27.)

One day while Enos was hunting in the forest, the things that he had learned from his father "sunk deep" into his heart. As you read the following verses, notice the importance of his father's teachings and the many action words that describe what was happening to Enos.

> Behold, it came to pass that I, Enos, knowing my father that he was a just man—for he taught me in his language, and

also in the nurture and admonition of the Lord—and blessed be the name of my God for it—

And I will tell you of the wrestle which I had before God, before I received a remission of my sins.

Behold, I went to hunt beasts in the forests; and the words which I had often heard my father speak concerning eternal life, and the joy of the saints, sunk deep into my heart.

And my soul hungered; and I kneeled down before my Maker, and I cried unto him in mighty prayer and supplication for mine own soul; and all the day long did I cry unto him; yea, and when the night came I did still raise my voice high that it reached the heavens.

And there came a voice unto me, saying: Enos, thy sins are forgiven thee, and thou shalt be blessed.

And I, Enos, knew that God could not lie; wherefore, my guilt was swept away. (Enos 1:1–6.)

Many times this same struggle takes place in the lives of our children as they face challenges such as going away to school, serving a mission, receiving a Church calling, or helping someone better understand the gospel. Our responsibility as parents is to teach them "concerning eternal life, and the joy of the saints," so that these teachings can sink deep into their hearts.

Sometimes we worry about peer pressure and the temptations of the world, and we underestimate the strength and power of our homes and of the word of God. We can receive great hope from two studies that were done in the early 1980s for the Church's Priesthood Executive Committee. The purpose of these studies was to help determine what led to young men's being ordained to the Melchizedek Priesthood, obtaining temple endowments, serving full-time missions, and being sealed in the temple.

Reporting on the findings of these two studies, an *Ensign* article stated that the second study showed "there were two factors which had the largest influence on whether young men desired to be morally clean, serve a mission, and marry in the temple. These were religious activity in the home (family prayer, family home evening, family scripture study), and agreement with parents on values and on goals for the future. In fact, these two things were found to have a greater influence than all other factors combined."

These studies also identified what we need to be helping our children do and warned us that activity in the Church is not enough. Drawing on conclusions made in the researchers' report, the *Ensign* article stated: "One of the results that needs to be achieved in a young man's life, the report points out, is consistent private religious behavior—personal prayer and scripture study, for example. Like most adolescents who are growing in maturity and learning to apply principles and practices in their lives, the survey [made in the second study] shows that 'many of the young men who are described as "active" do not engage in private forms of religious activity and are spiritually undernourished. There is a prevalent, but often deceptive sense among local leaders that "all is well" when they see youth participating in meetings and activities.' Though young men may attend and participate consistently, their private religious behavior is a far more reliable indicator of whether they will go on a mission or marry in the temple." (See *Ensign*, December 1984, pp. 66–68.)

These studies do not suggest that Church involvement and meeting attendance are not important. They simply found that family religious experiences are more important than all of the other Church programs combined. We become especially helpful to our children when we help them develop personal religious worship habits, such as meaningful personal prayer and daily scripture study. Personal worship cannot be forced but is effective only when it is done willingly by our children. One of the basic goals of our family home evenings and other family religious activities should be to help our children desire to study and pray on their own. It is important for us to honor their agency and to be patient with them as we encourage them through our own examples of personal prayer and scripture study.

What a blessing it is to realize the great impact we can have on our children's lives! If they are taught the gospel with love and with the Spirit, from the time they are young, most of them will not stray very far when they become older. Their personal feelings of worth and testimony will help them to overcome peer pressure and other negative pressures that they face as teenagers. Then, like Enos, there will be a time in their lives when they will say, "My parents taught me in the nurture and admonition of the Lord—and blessed be the name of my God for it."

Chapter 21

A DESIRE FOR THE
WELFARE OF MY BRETHREN

ENOS 1:5–9, 11

A young man who is active in the Church asked the following question: "I want to be obedient, but the thought of going on a
mission absolutely terrifies me. I'm no good at meeting people or
memorizing things or expressing myself. And I'm certainly no
salesman! Isn't there an alternative for good Mormon cowards?"

This young man's problem is not his fear or his feelings of inadequacy. Many people serve missions or accept other demanding
Church callings even though they have these same feelings. This
young man lacks testimony, faith, and an understanding of the
great gift of the Atonement. Once we come to appreciate the Savior and what he has done for us, we immediately begin to feel a desire to share the gospel with others. As we come to comprehend
the great power and love of God, we realize that he will help us
successfully do his work.

Enos is a good example of one who lived this principle. Notice
what leads to his great concern for the welfare of others:

> And there came a voice unto me, saying: Enos, thy sins are
> forgiven thee, and thou shalt be blessed.
> And I, Enos, knew that God could not lie; wherefore my
> guilt was swept away.
> And I said: Lord, how is it done?
> And he said unto me: Because of thy faith in Christ, whom
> thou has never before heard nor seen. And many years pass

away before he shall manifest himself in the flesh; wherefore, go to, thy faith hath made thee whole.

Now, it came to pass that when I had heard these words I began to feel a desire for the welfare of my brethren, the Nephites; wherefore, I did pour out my whole soul unto God for them. . . .

. . . [And] my faith began to be unshaken in the Lord; and I prayed unto him with many long strugglings for my brethren, the Lamanites. (Enos 1:5–9, 11.)

The sons of Mosiah felt the same desires for the souls of others as Enos, when they were converted and forgiven of their sins. Enos and the sons of Mosiah felt deep concern not only for their own people but for their enemies, as well. After their conversion the sons of Mosiah traveled throughout the land "striving to repair all the injuries which they had done to the church" and teaching the gospel to all those who would listen. After they had brought many Nephites to a "knowledge of their Redeemer," their hearts turned to the Lamanites. (See Mosiah 27:35–36.) The following verse reveals how strongly they felt about every human soul because of their own awakening to the importance of the Atonement and their joy in deliverance from sin: "Now they were desirous that salvation should be declared to every creature, for they could not bear that any human soul should perish; yea, even the very thoughts that any soul should endure endless torment did cause them to quake and tremble" (Mosiah 28:3).

The Lamanites were a "wild and a hardened and a ferocious people; a people who delighted in murdering the Nephites, and robbing and plundering them" (Alma 17:14). Enos said: "The people of Nephi did seek diligently to restore the Lamanites unto the true faith in God. But our labors were vain; their hatred was fixed, and they were led by their evil nature that they became wild, and ferocious, and a blood-thirsty people, full of idolatry and filthiness; feeding upon beasts of prey; dwelling in tents, and wandering about in the wilderness with a short skin girdle about their loins and their heads shaven; and their skill was in the bow, and in the cimeter, and the ax. And many of them did eat nothing save it was raw meat; and they were continually seeking to destroy us." (Enos 1:20.)

The fear and inadequacy that the sons of Mosiah must have felt as they contemplated preaching to the Lamanites were overcome by their great faith and their appreciation for the Savior's atonement. As we prepare young people to serve missions, maybe we need to spend less time talking about the responsibility of serving a mission and more time helping them to increase their testimonies and to better understand, appreciate, and accept the atonement of the Savior in their lives. As they feel the great joy and appreciation that comes as they grow spiritually, their hearts will automatically turn toward sharing the gospel with others. As discussed in the last chapter, when we encourage our children to do what leads to spiritual growth (such as personal prayer and scripture study), we help them to stay morally clean, serve missions, and marry in the temple.

Chapter 22

TRADITIONS OF
THEIR FATHERS

MOSIAH 1:5

An old rock church, built more than a hundred years ago in colonial America, had a woodburning stove built into one of its walls. Those who sat on the same side as the stove were always too hot, and those who sat on the opposite side were always too cold. To solve this problem, the services were stopped halfway through so that people could change sides.

When the church was eventually remodeled, the woodburning stove was covered over, and a modern heating system was installed. However, it had become such a strong tradition to shift sides of the room halfway through services that the ritual continued, even after the remodeling. Years later when the preacher was asked why he had stopped his service while the people moved to the opposite side of the room, he replied that he had no idea, other than it had been done for as long as anyone could remember.

This story demonstrates the power and strength that traditions can have on people's lives. When traditions are based on gospel principles and bring people closer to the Savior, they are good. When they lead us away from the truth, they are harmful. Traditions become dangerous when we follow them blindly without questioning their purpose or the effect they may be having on our lives. This is especially true if these traditions have been taught to us by our parents or other people whom we love and respect. Laman and Lemuel taught their children to hate the Nephites and to do everything they could to destroy them. Ultimately, millions of lives were negatively affected, both spiritually and physically, because two men started false traditions in their families.

These traditions kept the Lamanites from believing the scriptures and accepting the gospel. King Benjamin explained the effect these traditions had upon the Lamanite people: "Were it not for these things, which have been kept and preserved by the hand of God, that we might read and understand of his mysteries, and have his commandments always before our eyes, that even our fathers would have dwindled in unbelief, and we should have been like unto our brethren, the Lamanites, who know nothing concerning these things, or even do not believe them when they are taught them, *because of the traditions of their fathers*, which are not correct." (Mosiah 1:5, italics added.)

Because Satan realizes the great power that parents have over their children and future posterity, he works hard to get parents to teach or model incorrect traditions. The Lord works just as hard to inspire parents to instill correct traditions in the minds and hearts of their children. God warned us about Satan's methods of destroying our children when he said: "And that wicked one cometh and taketh away light and truth, through disobedience, from the children of men, and because of the tradition of their fathers. But I have commanded you to bring up your children in light and truth." (D&C 93:39–40.)

Joseph Smith wrote that much of the grief, tyranny, murder, and oppression of his day was "urged on and upheld by the influence of that spirit which hath so strongly riveted the creeds of the fathers, who have inherited lies, upon the hearts of the children" (D&C 123:7). He also received a revelation in which it is stated that many people who lived in the meridian of time "gave heed to the traditions of their fathers and believed not the gospel of Christ, wherein they became unholy" (D&C 74:4).

With these warnings in mind, each of us has the responsibility to evaluate the things we are teaching our families. We cannot afford to be content to accept, without question, the things that we have been taught by our parents or by others. Our goal is to keep and add to the truths that we have received and to discard any traditions or teachings that spiritually miss the mark. When we decide to reevaluate our lives and our traditions, we are simply admitting that none of us are perfect—including our parents and past teachers.

Just as important as eliminating false teachings and traditions from our lives is starting true traditions that will draw our families closer to the Savior and eventually lead them back to our Father in Heaven. There are so many good traditions that could be used as examples, but let's zero in on just one of them—the tradition of prayer.

One six-year-old boy was especially afraid to start school. On the first day, he would not leave his mother's side, and he was embarrassed that he was crying. His family was new to the area, and he lived a long way from the school. "He clung to [his mother's] hand as she led him into the empty school building and closed the door to one of the rooms. She put her arm around him and asked, 'Shall we ask Heavenly Father to help you today?' He nodded, and she quietly asked a blessing of the Lord upon her son. She prayed that he might enjoy the day, that he would find friends, and that he would be alert and receptive so he could learn. Just a few words, but the tears stopped. When they left the building he released her hand." (Marian P. Sorensen, *Ensign*, May 1973, p. 33.) This simple action by the mother, when accompanied by other similar actions, will develop a tradition of faith, love, and prayer that will guide this boy throughout his life.

Elder Matthew Cowley illustrated the result of this kind of teaching. He was a last-minute replacement for a speaker at a general conference who had been assigned to speak on the Book of Mormon. He gave a masterful talk and bore impressive testimony of this great book. Following the conference Sister Belle S. Spafford thanked him for his talk and said, "I marvel that you could give such a magnificent and convincing address with so little time in which to prepare!" Elder Cowley responded, "What do you mean by little time in which to prepare? I had plenty of time. I have had a lifetime. My preparation for that address began when I was a little boy at my mother's knee." (See Belle S. Spafford, *Women in Today's World* [Salt Lake City: Deseret Book Co., 1971], pp. 43–44.)

Prayer is just one example of a life-giving tradition that fills the lives of our children with purpose and direction. Other important traditions include such things as kindness, forgiveness, sustaining local and general leaders, keeping the Sabbath day holy, honoring the priesthood, doing home and visiting teaching, and giving unselfish service. These traditions will then be taught by our children to their children and so on until they have enriched the lives of generations to come.

Chapter 23

CHRIST ATONETH FOR CHILDREN

MOSIAH 3:16

Jesus demonstrated the great love he has for children when he visited the Nephite people: "He took their little children, *one by one*, and blessed them, and prayed unto the Father for them. And when he had done this he wept again; and he spake unto the multitude, and said unto them: Behold your little ones. And as they looked to behold they cast their eyes towards heaven, and they saw the heavens open, and they saw angels descending out of heaven as it were in the midst of fire; and they came down and encircled those little ones about, and they were encircled about with fire; and the angels did minister unto them." (3 Nephi 17:21–24, italics added.)

The scriptures are filled with evidence of the great love and concern God and Jesus Christ have for children. Jesus taught his disciples the importance of treating children with love and kindness when he said, "And whosoever shall offend one of these little ones that believe in me, it is better for him that a millstone were hanged about his neck, and he were cast into the sea" (Mark 9:42).

With the great concern that God has for children it is not surprising that payment for their transgressions is included in the Atonement. Although young children can't sin, because they have not learned and matured enough to always make correct decisions, all of them transgress commandments of God. Children do lie and argue and hit each other with their blocks. Most children have moments of selfishness and are sometimes even mean to one another.

But payment for these transgressions was covered in the suffering that Christ went through in Gethsemane.

King Benjamin taught this great truth when he declared, "And even if it were possible that little children could sin they could not be saved; but I say unto you they are blessed; for behold, as in Adam, or by nature, they fall, even so the blood of Christ atoneth for their sins" (Mosiah 3:16).

This great love that God has for children was beautifully manifest in an experience shared by Elder Thomas S. Monson. This story demonstrates the effort God will go through to bless just one child.

Christal was a young girl who lived in Louisiana. She lived on a ranch and was physically active until her body was attacked by cancer. First she lost her leg, and then the cancer moved into her lungs. After looking at a picture of the General Authorities, Christal randomly selected Elder Monson to give her a blessing, but she was too weak to travel to Salt Lake City. She was sure that the Lord would answer her prayer and have him sent to their stake conference so he would be able to bless her.

With no knowledge of Christal's desire, Church leaders made an inspired change in Elder Monson's conference schedule, and he was assigned to her area. After arriving in Louisiana, Elder Monson learned of Christal's situation, but because she lived some distance out of town, he felt he would not be able to visit her. The Spirit directed him otherwise, however. Early Sunday morning, in a spirit of fasting and prayer, Elder Monson arrived at Christal's home. Elder Monson described what happened on this special Sunday morning:

> Never have I felt more strongly the presence of the Lord than in the Methvin home. . . .
>
> The family surrounded Christal's bedside. I gazed down at a child who was too ill to rise—almost too weak to speak. Her illness had now rendered her sightless. So strong was the spirit that I fell to my knees, took her frail hand in mine, and said simply, "Christal, I am here." She parted her lips and whispered, "Brother Monson, I just knew you would come." I looked around the room. No one was standing. Each was on bended knee. A blessing was given. A faint smile crossed Christal's face. Her whispered "thank you" provided an appropriate benediction. . . .

Four days later . . . the pure spirit of Christal Methvin left its disease-ravaged body and entered the paradise of God. (*Ensign*, November 1975, pp. 20–22.)

God loves all children, and because of the Atonement, all children are alive in Christ, not needing repentance or baptism until they reach the age of accountability. It is our responsibility to help them understand, before the age of accountability, faith, repentance, prayer, obedience, the covenants of baptism, and the importance of listening to the Holy Ghost. This is so they can continue to take advantage of the atonement of Christ—through repentance and forgiveness—after they become accountable for their choices.

Chapter 24

I WILL
NOT SUCCOR

MOSIAH 7:28–29, 33

Sometimes we feel that, because of the great love that God has for us, he will bless us even though we have not been striving to keep his commandments. Sometimes people who have not even *thought* of God for years suddenly seek his help and expect immediate results. Most of us realize that these feelings are contrary to the word of God. If God blessed us for wickedness as well as righteousness, many who may otherwise have repented would still continue in their sins. God's blessings are withheld in times of wickedness because of his great love for us. Limhi's people provided a good example of this.

Limhi was a king over Nephite people who lived among the Lamanites. During the reign of King Noah they had become extremely wicked and had even killed the prophet Abinadi, who had been sent to call them to repentance. They had lost the blessings and protection of the Lord, and even though Limhi was a righteous king, they were in bondage to the Lamanites and had suffered many afflictions. Limhi gathered his people together and asked them: "Who wondereth that they [his people] are in bondage, and that they are smitten with sore afflictions? For behold, the Lord hath said: I will not succor my people in the day of their transgression; but I will hedge up their ways that they prosper not; and their doings shall be as a stumbling block before them." (Mosiah 7:28–29.)

If God had continued to bless Noah and Limhi's people, they

would never have turned to him and repented of their sins. Limhi told his people what they needed to do in order to receive help from the Lord and be freed from their bondage. He declared: "But if ye will turn to the Lord with full purpose of heart, and put your trust in him, and serve him with all diligence of mind, if ye do this, he will, according to his own will and pleasure, deliver you out of bondage" (Mosiah 7:33).

Notice that Limhi did not promise his people that they would be freed from their bondage immediately. If God blessed the people before they realized the great consequences of sin, they would quickly turn back to their evil ways. Blessings cannot be obtained just by saying we are sorry and we won't sin again. Talking about the Latter-day Saints in Missouri, the Lord said, "They were slow to hearken unto the voice of the Lord their God; therefore, the Lord their God is slow to hearken unto their prayers, to answer them in the day of their trouble" (D&C 101:7).

Not only do big sins affect the blessings we receive but our daily choices affect them as well. For instance, if we decide to go to an offensive movie, the Holy Ghost doesn't go in with us—and he doesn't wait outside the theater to start blessing us again once the movie is over. When we make choices that are offensive to the Spirit, we lose a portion of his companionship and influence, and it takes time and effort to regain these blessings. Help from the Lord cannot be turned on and off like a faucet. Elder Hartman Rector, Jr., warned: "Sometimes members appear to feel that fasting and prayer is all that is necessary to receive the answers to their problems. . . . It takes more than fasting and prayer. We must begin again; we must repent—confess and forsake our sins. We must study the scriptures, yea, search the scriptures; we must keep the commandments of God, and keep them precisely. For the commandments are calculated to get us in condition so that we can receive light and truth, even intelligence, which is communication from God, our Father, which we so desperately need." (*Ensign*, June 1971, p. 80.)

One of the great blessings of consistent faithfulness and obedience is that they enable us to receive the guidance of the Holy Ghost as problems arise. Strength, hope, guidance, inspiration, comfort, and other blessings of the Spirit can then come to us on a daily basis because our intentions are right and our hearts are pure.

Chapter 25

I SAW THAT
WHICH WAS GOOD

MOSIAH 9:1–2

The members of two Latter-day Saint branches wanted to do something special for Christmas, so they decided to prepare a variety show and present it to the inmates at a local prison. Anne N. Plumbly was one of these members, and she went along with mixed feelings because "all the inmates were reportedly serving terms for murder." Anne, who ended up having a very rewarding experience, shares what happened that day:

> As we stepped inside the gray walls of the prison . . . I thought of the inmates I imagined we would see—hard, cruel, ruthless men and I was afraid.
>
> How wrong my thoughts proved to be! Suddenly I was within a well-lighted hall. Sitting on the regimentally placed chairs were the prisoners. But where were the hardened criminals? All I could see were young men, mostly ages eighteen to perhaps thirty, but they did not have haunted looks nor signs of cruelty. . . .
>
> We presented our show, and as it drew to a close, we sang Christmas carols. The inmates were invited to sing with us. At this point I was nearly overcome with emotion. The men broke down, and some cried like lost children. A huge man at the rear of the hall sang his heart out, tears streaming down his face. (*Ensign*, April 1973, p. 44.)

Sometimes we have predetermined ideas about people or groups or situations that keep us from seeing the good in them. If you were a Nephite living in Book of Mormon times, it would have been easy to have preconceived ideas about the Lamanite people. These ideas could keep you from seeing or even looking for the good qualities that these people had. This is one reason why Zeniff was such an exceptional man. He was one of a group of Nephites who left Zarahemla and went to live in the land of Lehi-Nephi, which was possessed by the Lamanites. When they arrived on the borders of the land, Zeniff was sent as a spy to find out how they could destroy the Lamanites. As you read the following verses, notice the remarkable change that Zeniff experienced:

> I, Zeniff, having been taught in all the language of the Nephites, and having had a knowledge of the land of Nephi, or of the land of our fathers' first inheritance, and having been sent as a spy among the Lamanites that I might spy out their forces, that our army might come upon them and destroy them—*but when I saw that which was good among them* I was desirous that they should not be destroyed.
>
> Therefore, I contended with my brethren in the wilderness, for I would that our ruler should make a treaty with them; but he being an austere and a blood-thirsty man commanded that I should be slain; but I was rescued by the shedding of much blood. (Mosiah 9:1–2, italics added.)

Zeniff could see the good in the Lamanite people, and he put his life on the line to protect them. He teaches us a great lesson about looking for the good in others. Nearly everyone has some good, if we look for it, and by building on the good we may be able to help others become better. Very few stories demonstrate this principle better than the calling of a Maori named Syd to be the branch president for four hundred members of the Church in New Zealand. Syd had been inactive for many years, and when President Matthew Cowley visited him to make the call, he found Syd rocking on his front porch with a big cigar in his mouth. When President Cowley issued the call, Syd pulled the cigar out of his mouth and said, "You mean me and my cigar?"

President Cowley responded, "No, Syd—just you. We don't need your cigar."

Syd threw the cigar onto the ground, turned to President Cowley, and promised that he would keep the Word of Wisdom from that moment on. He said that he would serve as the branch president and that he would live the gospel and be worthy.

For many years, Syd was one of the strongest leaders in the mission. When the branch became a ward, his son became the first bishop. His grandson also eventually served as bishop of the ward. Syd's family is still giving great support and leadership to the Church in New Zealand. (See Glen L. Rudd, *Ensign,* January 1989, pp. 72–73.)

Hundreds of lives have been affected for the good because Heavenly Father and President Cowley saw the good in Syd. The same thing can take place around us as we look for—and see—the good in others. Many people have good hearts and will respond to the gospel if only they are approached properly.

You may have heard the thought that there is so much good in the worst of us and so much bad in the best of us that it's hard to tell which of us ought to be teaching the rest of us. There is a lot of truth to this statement, and as we look for the good in others we will consistently find it.

Chapter 26

YE HAVE ENTERED
INTO A COVENANT

MOSIAH 18:8–11

Grant had been home from his mission only a few weeks when he met and fell in love with Sandy. She returned his love, and they were married in the temple. There they made eternal covenants with each other and with God.

Two years later a son was born to them. They had anxiously awaited this great blessing, and they named him Allen. By this time their temple covenants had faded in their memory, and they were spending most of their time and effort in gathering material wealth. Between striving for new physical comforts and doing things with their new son, they gradually spent less and less time at church. They refused Church callings, quit paying their tithing, and eventually slipped into total inactivity. They spent most of their spare time with Allen, whom they loved very much. By this time their covenants were far from their minds.

Then their little son became seriously ill, and the doctors had no idea what the problem was. After many grief-filled days, Allen died. Grant and Sandy felt deep sorrow and even depression. One of the things that bothered them most was that they now remembered the covenants they had made in the temple and realized they had broken them. They were afraid that they would never see Allen again, and to make things worse they knew it would be their fault. After much agonizing soul-searching they realized that they had broken a sacred trust both with their Father in Heaven and with their own son.

After much anguish and prayer they decided to make their lives right with the Lord. They returned to full activity in the Church. When they were finally able to return to the temple, it meant so much more to them. They now realized the importance of their eternal covenants, and they knew how essential it was for them to keep the promises they had made.

As members of the Lord's church, we make many important covenants, but sometimes we don't contemplate how vital these covenants really are. All of these covenants are necessary and important to our future happiness. As we keep our part of these covenants, we can be assured that the Lord will also keep his. The covenants of baptism are made by every member of the Church.

We can learn a great deal about our baptismal covenants from the teachings of Alma the Elder. He had been a priest of wicked King Noah and was converted to the gospel after hearing the prophet Abinadi speak. Because Noah sought Alma's life, he taught the gospel secretly—in the wilderness at a place named Mormon. Two hundred and four people were baptized during the first gathering. Just before they were baptized, Alma explained to them the covenants they would be making:

> And it came to pass that he said unto them: Behold, here are the waters of Mormon (for thus were they called) and now, as ye are desirous to come into the fold of God, and to be called his people, and are willing to bear one another's burdens, that they may be light;
>
> Yea, and are willing to mourn with those that mourn; yea, and comfort those that stand in need of comfort, and to stand as witnesses of God at all times and in all things, and in all places that ye may be in, even until death, that ye may be redeemed of God, and be numbered with those of the first resurrection, that ye may have eternal life—
>
> Now I say unto you, if this be the desire of your hearts, what have you against being baptized in the name of the Lord, as a witness before him that ye have entered into a covenant with him, that ye will serve him and keep his commandments, that he may pour out his Spirit more abundantly upon you?
>
> And now when the people had heard these words, they clapped their hands for joy, and exclaimed: This is the desire of our hearts. (Mosiah 18:8–11.)

As we read this passage carefully we can find at least five important covenants that we make when we are baptized. Let's take a closer look at these five baptismal covenants:

1. *"As ye are desirous to come into the fold of God, and to be called his people"*—To take upon ourselves the name of Christ and be called Christians is a sacred responsibility. More specifically, we are members of The Church of Jesus Christ of Latter-day Saints, which is the Savior's organization here upon the earth. The things we do and say and the way we treat others have a direct bearing on how others may feel about the Savior's church and, therefore, how they feel about him.

2. *"Are willing to bear one another's burdens, that they may be light; yea, and are willing to mourn with those that mourn; yea, and comfort those that stand in need of comfort"*—This was a very important promise for those who listened to Alma because not only did they have the normal spiritual, social, and emotional needs that all of us have today, but they faced physical persecution as well. Part of our responsibility, as representatives of Christ, is to reach out to members and nonmembers alike.

3. *"To stand as witnesses of God at all times and in all things, and in all places that ye may be in, even until death"*—What a beautiful way of reminding us that we do represent Christ and his kingdom here upon the earth! Our fulfillment of this promise takes courage and sensitivity—and it encompasses the other four promises that we make. We "stand as witnesses of God" when we remember that we carry the name of Christ and demonstrate the same compassion and love to others that Christ demonstrated.

4. *"Ye have entered into a covenant with him, that ye will serve him"*—King Benjamin taught us that we serve God when we serve others. This includes informal service that we give daily as we see and try to fulfill the needs of those we come in contact with. It also includes our willingness to formally serve in Church callings that give us opportunities to strengthen and bless the lives of those we are called to serve.

5. *"And keep his commandments"*—The best way to take upon us the name of Christ and to stand as witnesses of God at all times is to keep the commandments. A lack of obedience hurts not only us but those around us as well. The obedience of each individual member of the Church slows down or speeds up the work of the Lord and the growth of the kingdom of God. This was demonstrated well by a young man named Brent Turek:

In 1963 Brent Turek was the star on Panguitch High School's basketball team, which had lost only one game all season. When a reporter and photographer for *Sports Illustrated* came all the way from the east to visit him at his home in the little town of Hatch, Utah, Brent still knew he had to make the correct choices. Instead of cancelling his appointment to go ward teaching, Brent invited the reporter and photographer to accompany him. When the article on the Panguitch basketball team came out in *Sports Illustrated*, Brent's picture was not a fast-moving basketball shot, but a picture of him as a ward teacher, giving the Lord's message to one of his assigned families. (Robert L. Goodrich, comp., *Instructor*, January 1968, p. 37.)

The Lord has promised us that as we keep our covenants he will forgive our sins; bless us with the companionship of the Holy Ghost; and eventually bestow upon us eternal life, the greatest of all the gifts of God. It is important, as Grant and Sandy came to realize, to remember the sacred covenants that we have made and to pray daily for the strength and guidance to keep them.

Chapter 27

HE HAS PRAYED
MUCH CONCERNING THEE

MOSIAH 27:14

Most of us pray for someone besides ourselves almost every time we pray. We pray that some person will be healed, or accept the gospel, or know that he is loved. We ask God to bless others with comfort, or with strength, or with the guidance of the Holy Ghost. Sometimes, when a loved one is rebelling, or facing some crisis, or is far away from home, prayer is one of the few ways we have of helping him. The scriptures and the living prophets have assured us many times that these prayers are not in vain.

The conversion of Alma the Younger illustrates this as well as any story in the scriptures. Along with the sons of Mosiah, he had been causing great havoc in the Church. Then one day an angel appeared to him and commanded him to stop his persecution of the Church. The reason for the angel's coming should be a testimony to all of us that God will hearken to our faith and prayers. The angel declared to Alma: "Behold, the Lord hath heard the prayers of his people, and also the prayers of his servant, Alma, who is thy father; for he has prayed with much faith concerning thee that thou mightest be brought to the knowledge of the truth; therefore, for this purpose have I come to convince thee of the power and authority of God, that the prayers of his servants might be answered according to their faith" (Mosiah 27:14).

God does not usually send an angel in answer to our prayers for wayward loved ones, but because of our faith and righteousness he does pour out his Spirit more abundantly both on the loved one and on those that may be able to help. The important thing is never to give up. Elder Loren C. Dunn pleaded: "Oh, parents, no matter what the difficulty, may we never desert our children in some dark and dangerous thoroughfare of life, no matter what prompted them to get there. When they reach the point—and for some it may be a painfully long time—when they reach the point that they need us, I pray that we might not let them down." (*Improvement Era*, December 1970, p. 64.)

Because our children and other loved ones have their agency, the Lord will not force them to follow him. He will, however, bless us for our efforts and pour out blessings upon them if they will only respond.

Up to now our discussion has centered mostly on those who are reacting negatively to the gospel, but many of our prayers will be for those who are trying to live the gospel. We often pray for Church leaders, missionaries and students away from home, those who are coping with death or serious illness, and friends and neighbors who are traveling. These prayers are as important and as effective as those that are offered for the rebellious. The following story, about a young man called on a mission to Tonga illustrates the great power that can come as we pray for others.

The mission president had put this young Elder on a boat to Fiji and had told him that he would be met when he arrived. However, when the boat docked no one was there to meet him. Since he had no visa, ticket, or money, he found himself stranded in the "customs shed."

As evening came and it became dark, most of the workers left for home. The Elder was hungry and very scared, since he had no idea what was going to happen to him. He tried to get some rest by lying down on the rough cement floor. In desperation, he cried out to God, asking him what he should do. He later explained how God answered his prayer:

> I felt almost transported. I didn't see anything or hear anything, in a physical sense; but, in a more real way, I saw a family in far-off Idaho kneeling together in prayer; and I heard my mother, acting as mouth, say as clearly as anything can be heard, "And bless John on his mission."

As that faithful family called down the powers of heaven to bless their missionary son in a way they could not physically do, I testify that the powers of heaven did come down, and they lifted me up and, in a spiritual way, allowed me, for a brief moment, to once again join that family circle in prayer. I was one with them. I was literally swallowed up in the love and concern of a faithful family. . . .

Tears of joy flowed freely as I had restored to me the warmth of security, the light of love, and the strength of hope. And when I again felt the hard, uneven cement beneath me, there was no fear, no sorrow, no trepidation, only deep gratitude and certain assurance.

It was only a few minutes later that two elders showed up and rescued this young missionary. (See John H. Groberg, *Ensign*, May 1982, pp. 51–52.)

As this family prayed for their missionary they had no idea what his specific needs were, but Heavenly Father knew, and he fulfilled those needs. All of us know people who need God's help and direction in some way. There are almost as many different kinds of needs as there are people. As we kneel in sincere prayer and pray with real intent, God will respond to our prayers. He may not always bless those we pray for by giving them what *we* think they need; rather, he will bless them in the way that will benefit them the most.

Chapter 28

BROUGHT UPON THEMSELVES THE CURSE

ALMA 3:18–19, 27

None of us came to this earth against our will. We were allowed the agency to choose, and we shouted for joy when the opportunity to come here was presented to us. Now that we are here it is up to us to wisely use the time and agency that have been allotted to us. President Spencer W. Kimball explained that since eternal life "is a cooperative program to be developed by the Lord and his offspring on earth[, it] thus becomes the overall responsibility of man to cooperate fully with the Eternal God in accomplishing this objective" (*The Miracle of Forgiveness* [Salt Lake City: Bookcraft, 1969], p. 2).

Since this earth life is meant for us, when we sin, we sin not only against God but also against ourselves. All sins are self-defeating and keep us from becoming what we came here to be. The commandments of God are not stumbling blocks that have been placed in our way to test us, but they are stepping stones that help us develop the attributes and character traits of God. When we break the commandments, we slow down our own progress, and no one is to blame but ourselves.

Alma explained this principle two thousand years ago as he taught his people about the Amlicites. The curse that fell upon them is the curse that falls upon all of us if we rebel instead of cooperating with our Father in Heaven. It is the curse of losing his guidance and influence and of eventually being cut off from his presence: "They had come out in open rebellion against God;

therefore it was expedient that the curse should fall upon them. Now I would that ye should see that they brought upon themselves the curse; and even so doth every man that is cursed bring upon himself his own condemnation. . . . For every man receiveth wages of him whom he listeth to obey, and this according to the words of the spirit of prophecy; therefore let it be according to the truth." (Alma 3:18–19, 27.)

Samuel, the great Lamanite prophet, taught very clearly that when we sin, we sin against ourselves: "And now remember, re- member, my brethren, that whosoever perisheth, perisheth unto himself; and whosoever doeth iniquity, doeth it unto himself; for behold, ye are free; ye are permitted to act for yourselves; for be- hold, God hath given unto you a knowledge and he hath made you free" (Helaman 14:30).

Many stories could be shared concerning those who have made incorrect choices and brought upon themselves unhappy consequences. All of us have made such choices during our lives. Some blame others—or God—for their problems and sink even deeper into depression and sin, while others take full responsibility for the choices they have made and try to rectify their mistakes. The following story not only depicts the sorrow that follows sin but also demonstrates the peace and feelings of self-worth that come as we accept responsibility for our actions and do things the Lord's way.

A Brigham Young University student, who really needed the money, found a wallet in a phone booth and kept it. She justified her act at first, but soon her conscience began to work on her. She was never able to throw the wallet away, and nine years later she still had the wallet—and much spiritual conflict. One day, as she looked through the wallet for the hundredth time, she found a piece of paper that she had never seen before and which helped her trace the wallet's owner. She called the woman and asked her if she could return the wallet to her. The owner of the wallet explained their special meeting as follows:

> As though she had rehearsed this experience in her mind a hundred times, she reached out her steady hand, looked me squarely in the eye, and handed me the wallet. Her steady gaze reflected the radiance of a good and honest life.
>
> Then her eyes dropped as she whispered, "Will you please forgive me? I want to be honest." Words would not come. I

could only reach for her hand and nod affirmatively. From my office, I watched her walk away from my desk and out the front door. . . .

I went to the window to watch her with her shoulders square, head erect, and with a lilt in her step as she turned the corner out of sight. (Ardeth G. Kapp, *New Era*, July 1976, pp. 7–9.)

When this woman took the wallet, she sinned much more against herself than against the owner of the wallet. As she made the decision to make a real effort to make things right, she blessed herself much more than anyone else. We are here on earth not just to please God but to become like him. As we do things that take us away from God, we damn ourselves and the purpose for which we came here. As we do things that bring us closer to God, we feel peace, joy, satisfaction, and self-worth.

Chapter 29

WICKEDNESS WAS A STUMBLING-BLOCK

ALMA 4:10

Elder James E. Talmage told the story of a lamp peddler who claimed that his lamps were far superior to other lamps of his day. Elder Talmage felt somewhat skeptical and invited the salesman to compare his lamp to the one he already owned.

As Elder Talmage lit his well-trimmed lamp, the lamp salesman praised it and said it was excellent. The salesman then lit the lamp he was selling. Elder Talmage said of it: "Its light made bright the remotest corner of my room. In its brilliant blaze my own little Argand wick burned a weak, pale yellow. Until that moment of convincing demonstration I had never known the dim obscurity in which I had lived and labored, studied and struggled." Elder Talmage immediately bought the lamp. That same night he took it to his laboratory and found that it was four times as bright as his old one.

Elder Talmage then compared this story to missionary work by saying: "The man who would sell me a lamp did not disparage mine. He placed his greater light alongside my feebler flame, and I hastened to obtain the better.

"The missionary servants of the Church of Jesus Christ today are sent forth, not to assail nor ridicule the beliefs of men, but to set before the world a superior light, by which the smoky dimness of the flickering flames of man-made creeds shall be apparent." (*Improvement Era*, January 1914, pp. 256–58.)

The Lord has asked us to "arise and shine forth, that [our] light may be a standard for the nations" (D&C 115:5). As we show what the gospel has done for us and our families, others will desire to make the gospel a part of their lives. There are many men and women who do not realize that they are living in darkness, and when they see the light that is available to them, they will "haste to obtain" it.

The growth of God's church and kingdom here upon the earth is dependent on how well each one of us becomes a "lamp" for the Lord and for his gospel. The Savior said that when we let our light shine others see our good works and desire to glorify our Heavenly Father (see Matthew 5:16).

The opposite is also true. If our own lights are dim, the rest of the world remains in darkness and our lack of light causes others to stumble. This was a problem that Alma faced—one that even caused him to resign as the chief judge so that he could devote all of his time to the ministry. Many members of the Church had become proud and were contending with nonmembers and members alike. They had even begun to "smite one another with their fists." It became a cause of much trial and affliction for the Church. (See Alma 1:21–23.) The Book of Mormon record explains that "the wickedness of the church was a great stumbling-block to those who did not belong to the church; and thus the church began to fail in its progress" (Alma 4:10).

I have, in my home, a dining-room light fixture that contains many small bulbs. It is amazing how much the light decreases when just one of these bulbs burns out. So it is with the Church. Each one of us is a light bearer for the Savior, and each one of us is important. If enough of us allowed our lights to flicker and grow dim, the whole Church would be affected. Some of us, because we have had the light of the gospel in our lives for many years, have forgotten how dark the world is without this great source of truth and direction. We sometimes do not comprehend how much we further the work of Christ and influence those around us simply by living the gospel and radiating the light that we have been blessed with.

President N. Eldon Tanner told a humorous story about a young boy who had invited several friends to a party. It was scheduled to be held outside, but the weather turned bad and the boys moved indoors. As the noise level reached greater and greater intensity, the mother came up with an idea. She announced a contest to see which boy could make the ugliest face. A prize would even be given to the winner.

After the boys had practiced for several minutes, the father came in to select the winner. He walked around the room looking carefully at each boy until he finally said that he was ready to announce his decision. He then stopped in front of one of the boys and said, "You are the winner." The surprised boy replied, "But I wasn't even playing."

President Tanner then summed up the great effect each of us has on others, even though we might not realize it: "So it is with us as members of the Church. We may not even be working at trying to make conversions, or influencing people, but often they are watching us and judging the Church by our actions. Let each of us so live as to be valiant in the cause of truth and righteousness, and let our light so shine before men that they will see our good works and be led to investigate the gospel truths which we espouse." (*Ensign*, January 1979, p. 4.)

It is impossible for us to go through a normal day without influencing someone for either good or ill. As we interact with others, whether we like it or not, judgments are made, impressions are formed, and ideas are planted. As we live the gospel we receive the Holy Ghost and radiate a spirit of optimism, joy, and love—all of which have a positive effect on those we associate with. Many of them will desire the light that they see we have and "haste to obtain" it.

Chapter 30

BEARING DOWN
IN PURE TESTIMONY

ALMA 4:19

Parley P. Pratt wrote that while he was visiting with Joseph
Smith in Philadelphia,

> a very large church was opened for him to preach in, and about
> three thousand people assembled to hear him. Brother Rigdon
> spoke first, and dwelt on the Gospel, illustrating his doctrine by
> the Bible. When he was through, brother Joseph arose like a
> lion about to roar; and being full of the Holy Ghost, spoke in
> great power, bearing testimony of the visions he had seen, the
> ministering of angels which he had enjoyed; and how he had
> found the plates of the Book of Mormon, and translated them
> by the gift and power of God. He commenced by saying: "If no-
> body else had the courage to testify of so glorious a message
> from Heaven, and of the finding of so glorious a record, he felt
> to do it in justice to the people, and leave the event with God."
>
> The entire congregation were astounded; electrified, as it
> were, and overwhelmed with the sense of the truth and power
> by which he spoke, and the wonders which he related. A last-
> ing impression was made; many souls were gathered into the
> fold. And I bear witness, that he, by his faithful and powerful
> testimony, cleared his garments of their blood. (*Autobiography
> of Parley P. Pratt* [Salt Lake City: Deseret Book Co., 1938], pp.
> 298–99.)

This account by Brother Pratt demonstrates the great difference in potency and effectiveness between teaching the gospel with logic and bearing fervent testimony with the power of the Spirit. I had the opportunity to serve as a missionary in Australia under Elder Bruce R. McConkie, who taught us the importance of testifying by the Spirit. Baptisms doubled as we put this principle into practice.

It is very apparent that Alma understood the power of pure testimony. He was both chief judge over the people and high priest over the Church. However, because of the wickedness of the people, he "retained the office of high priest unto himself; but he delivered the judgment-seat unto Nephihah. And this he did that he himself might go forth among his people, or among the people of Nephi, that he might preach the word of God unto them, to stir them up in remembrance of their duty, and that he might pull down, by the word of God, all the pride and craftiness and all the contentions which were among his people, seeing no way that he might reclaim them save it were in *bearing down in pure testimony* against them." (Alma 4:18–19, italics added.)

In a matter of just two years most of the branches of the Church were strengthened as thousands of members and non-members of the Church responded to Alma's testimony. Sometimes we overlook this great power and, consequently, we don't share our testimony enough with family members, friends and neighbors, and those we serve in the Church.

A teenage girl had an experience that taught her the great power that can accompany sincere testimony. When this girl was baptized her nonmember mother cursed her. Each time she participated in Church activities her mother yelled at her and called her loathsome and degrading names. Once she had an opportunity to go to the temple with other young people. As she left her home her mother continued her past behavior by swearing at her and telling her that she was no daughter of hers.

After the group had finished several baptismal sessions the temple president invited them into his office, where he talked to them about their own baptisms. He told these young people that the Holy Ghost would guide and bless them if they were worthy. Then he said, "If anyone should oppose you, or bring harm to you, you can overcome that opposition by the influence of the Holy Ghost."

At about this time the temple president noticed that the young girl was crying. She shared with him the situation that she faced at home: "I have been fasting ever since I left home that here in the temple I would be given a guide and the power to overcome the opposition of my mother. I was going away disappointed. But now, at the last moment, you have given me the key. I am going to bring Mother within the influence of the power of the Holy Ghost which I have a right to enjoy."

When the girl arrived at her home her mother greeted her in her usual manner, but this time the girl did not fight back. Instead she put her arm around her mother's shoulder and led her over to the couch. As they sat down she put her cheek next to her mother's and bore her testimony. After bearing her testimony she told her mother about the wonderful time she had had in the temple. Her mother broke into tears and asked her to forgive her. When the girl wrote the temple president a few weeks later, her mother was preparing for baptism. (See Harold B. Lee, *New Era*, February 1971, p. 4.)

When the bearing of testimony is accompanied by the power of the Holy Ghost, the message is carried into the hearts of those we are speaking to. The Holy Ghost will inspire us to know when to bear our testimonies and what to say. Just as pure testimony had a great effect on the Nephite people and caused many of them to repent of their sins, it can have the same effect on many of those we care about today. As we make testimony bearing an integral part of our teaching, whether it be at home, in church, or with friends who are not members of the Church, we will come to appreciate even more the great power of the Spirit in the conversion process.

Chapter 31

TOUCH NOT
THEIR UNCLEAN THINGS

ALMA 5:57

Most of us become somewhat upset when we find insects, hair, or other foreign matter in our food or drink. Many times, even though the distasteful object could easily be removed, we discard whatever food or drink is remaining. We sometimes even feel nauseated as our minds quickly imagine the awful creatures or things we may have already devoured unknowingly. We should be concerned about the cleanliness of the food we allow into our physical bodies; but we should be even more concerned about the food we allow into our minds and hearts.

Most of us have heard of the "garbage in, garbage out" equation. In a lecture given to seminary teachers, Latter-day Saint musician Lex de Azevedo proposed two other equations:

$$TS = TT = TB = TK$$

Telestial Stimuli = Telestial Thoughts
Telestial Thoughts = Telestial Behavior
Telestial Behavior = Telestial Kingdom

$$CS = CT = CB = CK$$

Celestial Stimuli = Celestial Thoughts
Celestial Thoughts = Celestial Behavior
Celestial Behavior = Celestial Kingdom

Alma taught his people the importance of avoiding telestial stimuli: "And now I say unto you, all you that are desirous to follow the voice of the good shepherd, come ye out from the wicked, and be ye separate, and *touch not their unclean things*" (Alma 5:57, italics added).

The Lord told us the same thing in our day when he said: "Go ye out from among the wicked. Save yourselves. Be ye clean that bear the vessels of the Lord." (D&C 38:42.)

We are besieged with off-color or crude jokes, television shows, movies, videos, books, and magazines. If we allow or even invite these words and pictures into our lives, they will pollute our minds and hearts. Bishop H. Burke Peterson warned us of these evil influences:

> Our mind, which is like a tremendous reservoir itself, is capable of taking in whatever it may be fed—good and bad, trash and garbage, as well as righteous thoughts and experiences. As we go through life, we may be exposed to stories, pictures, books, jokes, and language that are filthy and vulgar, or to television shows and movies that are not right for us to see or hear. Our mind will take it all in. It has a capacity to store whatever we will give it. Unfortunately, what our mind takes in, it keeps—sometimes forever. It's a long, long process to cleanse a mind that has been polluted by unclean thoughts. . . .
>
> Evil acts are preceded by unrighteous thoughts. And unrighteous thoughts are born of vulgar stories, jokes, pictures, conversation, and a myriad of other satanic products. (*Ensign*, November 1980, p. 38.)

We do not need to partake of the spiritual pollution the world offers us. With the help of the Holy Ghost we can fill our lives with things of beauty and great worth. There are many movies, programs, books, and plays that educate and inspire. It is simply a matter of choice. As we invite celestial stimuli into our lives we develop celestial thoughts and actions. Talking about our time, the Lord assured us that we can live celestial lives in this telestial world when he prophesied that his followers would "stand in holy places and . . . not be moved" (D&C 45:32).

Chapter 32

HOW TO SUCCOR
HIS PEOPLE

ALMA 7:11–12

When we are faced with difficult situations in our lives we can turn with confidence to the Savior both because of his great love and kindness and because he truly understands how we feel. President Ezra Taft Benson taught that Jesus "possesses all the attributes of the divine nature of God. He is virtuous, patient, kind, long-suffering, gentle, meek, and charitable. If we are weak or deficient in any of these qualities, He stands willing to strengthen and compensate. . . . Indeed there is no human condition—be it suffering, incapacity, inadequacy, mental deficiency, or sin—which He cannot comprehend or for which His love will not reach out to the individual." (*Ensign*, June 1990, pp. 5–6.)

Alma taught these same principles in a beautiful way when he explained: "And he shall go forth, suffering pains and afflictions and temptations of every kind; and this that the word might be fulfilled which saith he will take upon him the pains and the sicknesses of his people. And he will take upon him death, that he may loose the bands of death which bind his people; and he will take upon him their infirmities, that his bowels may be filled with mercy, according to the flesh, that he may know according to the flesh how to succor his people according to their infirmities." (Alma 7:11–12.)

We feel that we know what we need, but the Savior comprehends what our true needs are. Sometimes we are looking for the solution to an immediate problem while the Savior is trying to help us develop the strength and wisdom to solve or avoid many future problems and to become more like him. A few years ago a Church leader and his wife registered for a Book of Mormon symposium at Brigham Young University. This was a three-day workshop, which meant they would be staying two nights at the university.

The day before the symposium started their four-year-old boy developed a high fever. Since there was no way they could go if one of their children was sick, they prayed that he would be made well. They felt that because it was for a good cause, God would respond. After all, they were sure he would want them to attend the symposium and learn more about the Book of Mormon. They prayed several times during the day and gave their son a blessing, but he did not improve. When he went to bed he still had a very high temperature. The parents felt very frustrated, and the father even felt angry. He couldn't understand why God wouldn't intercede when they were trying to do something that was good.

Each hour, they went into their son's room and checked his temperature, but to no avail. As the father knelt down at about midnight to plead with the Lord again, the Holy Ghost touched his spirit, and he realized that his attitude had been wrong. He knew in his heart that he had been demanding a blessing because he felt he knew what was best. He was flooded with feelings of embarrassment and humility as he thought about the anger he had felt when his prayers had not been answered.

He asked God to forgive him, and he told Heavenly Father how much he and his wife had been looking forward to learning more about the Book of Mormon. He admitted that God knew what was best and told him that if he wanted them to stay home, it would be fine with them. They wanted to do whatever God desired. Tears flowed down his cheeks onto the bedspread as he closed his prayer.

Even though he had checked his son just before praying, he felt prompted to check him again. This time the boy's temperature was normal, and he knew that his prayer had been answered. He also realized that it had not been answered earlier because the Lord had wanted him to learn a great lesson about humility and prayer.

Jesus understands our true needs and will help us fulfill these needs as we approach him in humility and with complete trust in his judgment. Sometimes we may not receive what we ask for, but we will always receive what we really need—for he knows how best to succor his people.

Chapter 33

WATCH AND PRAY
CONTINUALLY

ALMA 13:28

Talking about the conditions that we face in today's world, President Marion G. Romney declared, "I am persuaded that nothing short of the guidance of the Holy Spirit can bring us through safely." After indicating that he did not want us to be discouraged but that he did want us to recognize the challenges we face, he said:

> Personally, I am not disheartened. I am concerned, but I do not live in terror. It has been said that the late President J. Golden Kimball once attended a stake conference session in which the speaker who preceded him occupied nearly all the time with a scorching call to repentance, and that when Brother J. Golden followed him, he simply said, "Well, brothers and sisters, I suppose the best thing for all of us to do is to go home and commit suicide."
>
> Serious as are our times, however, I do not recommend Brother Golden's prescribed course, because I have an unwavering confidence that if we will heed and follow the guidance of the Holy Spirit, the Lord can and will preserve and bring us through safely. (*Ensign*, January 1980, p. 2.)

President Romney clearly teaches that we cannot successfully navigate this life without the help of the Holy Ghost. Sometimes, if we are not very careful, we will find ourselves thinking that we can live the gospel on our own—that it is simply a matter of self-control. This feeling is absolutely false and may come from Satan or from misguided pride. Some of our habits and traits are so ingrained that we cannot overcome them without the help of our Father in Heaven.

One Church member who failed to overcome sin using the willpower-only approach shared the following insight: "A big part of my problem . . . was that I saw my sins as a kind of contest—them against me. I thought I had to struggle, to fight against them, that righteousness was a matter of willpower. . . . The outcome of this attempt at righteousness . . . was that most of my sins were still with me, and one or two were worse than when I had started. I was discouraged. I had seen myself clearly; I had faced my sins. But I hadn't been able to get rid of them. I was left with a view of myself as essentially a failure." (A. Lynn Scorseby, *Ensign*, January 1980, p. 55.)

Many of us share these same feelings when we decide that we will use our great willpower and never sin again. We will never lie again, or yell at the children again, or lose our temper again. Alma gave us the key to overcoming sin and developing righteousness: "Humble yourselves before the Lord, and call on his holy name, and *watch and pray continually*, that ye *may not be tempted above that which ye can bear*, and thus be led by the Holy Spirit, becoming humble, meek, submissive, patient, full of love, and all long-suffering" (Alma 13:28, italics added).

Notice that the great qualities of humility, meekness, submissiveness, patience, love, and long-suffering come to us as we watch and pray continually. They come when we work hard to develop these qualities, invite things into our lives that will help these qualities grow, and pray continually for the Lord to give us the guidance and strength that we need.

President Spencer W. Kimball taught the importance of prayer in overcoming sin: "When I used to travel throughout the stakes and missions of the Church in earlier years, I often met people who were in trouble or who had great need. My first question to them was, 'What about your prayers? How often? How deeply involved are you when you pray?' I have observed that sin generally comes when communication lines are down." (*Ensign*, October 1981, p. 3.)

The great power of prayer in conquering sin was confirmed by a young man who was preparing to join the Church. He and his wife both used tobacco, but following the Word of Wisdom lesson they decided together to give up smoking. He was not concerned about his own ability to quit, because he had already quit several times just to prove to himself that he could. His concern was for his wife, who had never tried to quit before. He was surprised when just the opposite took place:

> His wife quit without any apparent difficulty, but he had tremendous difficulty. He became nervous and irritable. He could not rest. He was cranky among his fellow workers. He could not sleep at night. But inasmuch as his wife had quit, he was not going to be outdone by her. So, one night, he became so restless, so disturbed that he could not sleep, and his wife suggested to him that he pray about it. He thought that was a good joke. He ridiculed the idea of prayer; he said, "This is something I have to do. Nobody can help me with this. I can do this." But as the night passed, and he had done everything he could to stimulate sleep and rest without any success, finally in despair he humbled himself enough to kneel at the side of the bed and pray vocally. According to his own testimony, he said that he got up from his prayer, got into bed, went to sleep, and has never been tempted by cigarets since. He has absolutely lost the taste for tobacco. He said, "The Word of Wisdom was not a health program for me. It was a lesson on humility." (Eldred G. Smith, *Improvement Era*, June 1955, p. 405.)

Because this young man had done all he could do and had humbled himself before the Lord and called on his holy name, the Lord would not allow him to be tempted above that which he could bear. Therefore his desire for tobacco was taken from him. The Lord has promised all of us that none of us will be "tempted above that [we] are able; but will with the temptation also make a way to escape, that [we] may be able to bear it" (1 Corinthians 10:13). The way most of us will avoid or overcome temptation is through personal effort, humility, and constant, fervent prayer.

Chapter 34

BE PATIENT
IN AFFLICTIONS

ALMA 17:11

As the sons of Mosiah and their companions journeyed toward the land of the Lamanites, they fasted and prayed much that they might receive the Spirit of the Lord so that they could be successful missionaries. They received not only the Lord's Spirit but also the following instructions and promise: "And the Lord said unto them also: Go forth among the Lamanites, thy brethren, and establish my word; yet ye shall be *patient in long-suffering and afflictions, that ye may show forth good examples* unto them in me, and I will make an instrument of thee in my hands unto the salvation of many souls" (Alma 17:11, italics added).

When we or the Church are verbally attacked, sometimes our first impulse is to fight back. Since contention is of the devil (see 3 Nephi 11:29), fighting back is the very thing he wants us to do. When we contend we lose the Lord's Spirit and become very much like those we are contending with. We waste our time "playing defense" instead of continuing to "score" through gospel living and dedicated Church service. When we argue with others they become enemies instead of friends and they try even harder to put us or the Church down, because they can no longer admit they are wrong without losing face.

In 1983 the First Presidency counseled us on how we should respond to inaccurate or critical information about the Church. They wrote that much of the information given on television and radio, as well as in newspapers and magazines, was "accurate and favorable," but that some was not. They also pointed out that "in areas where opposition has been particularly intense, the growth of the Church has actually been hastened rather than retarded." The First Presidency further stated: "We do not think it either wise or appropriate to react to all criticisms nor to challenge those responsible for them. Nor is it wise to enter into debates with them either individually or before audiences. However, when opportunities arise to present our message which do not involve contention or debate, we suggest you take advantage of them." The First Presidency also suggested that we respond in positive ways, explain the high standards of the Church, and, above all, "bear testimony of the restoration of the gospel and that Jesus is the Christ." (See *Church News*, December 18, 1983, p. 2.)

When Elder Marvin J. Ashton visited a South Pacific island, some of the missionaries were eagerly awaiting his arrival so they could show him an anti-Mormon pamphlet that contained false and slanderous statements against the Church. They waited quietly as he read the malicious literature and was then asked, "What do we do now? How can we best counteract such lies?"

The answer he gave is excellent counsel for when we are attacked personally as well as for when the attack is directed against the Church. He said, "To the author of these words, we do nothing. We have no time for contention. We only have time to be about our Father's business. Contend with no man. Conduct yourselves as gentlemen with calmness and conviction and I promise you success." (*Ensign*, May 1978, p. 7.)

In a small community in Utah, a local Christian group held anti-Mormon classes every Tuesday evening. The young people in the area were taught lies and half-truths concerning the Church and were given scriptures that could be used to combat the Church. Some of these young people were very vocal and active in teaching against the Church, especially among their friends at school.

One young man managed to stir up several Latter-day Saint youth, who in turn brought him to the seminary during lunchtime so that the seminary teacher would dispute his claims and discredit him. After the young man had finished vocalizing his criticisms against the Church, the Latter-day Saint teenagers expected the teacher to pounce on him and to reveal to all concerned his great stupidity. Instead the teacher told the young man how much he appreciated his courage in coming and talking with him. He congratulated him on the time he had spent studying the Bible and putting together his arguments. He then simply told the young man that he loved him and then shared with him his testimony of the gospel. He especially stressed the importance of a living prophet and of the Book of Mormon. He then asked the young man to learn more about the Church by reading the Book of Mormon and praying about it. The young man and the teacher shook hands and parted good friends. That fall the young man was enrolled in seminary, where he learned a great deal more about the Church.

The sons of Mosiah were patient in the afflictions that they received, and eventually they had the opportunity to teach and baptize thousands of Lamanites. As we patiently and lovingly do our best to correct false accusations by teaching the truth in a spirit of meekness and love, those who honestly seek the truth will respond to the gospel.

Chapter 35

I WILL BE
THY SERVANT

ALMA 17:25

Elder Allen had been on his mission only two weeks, and he was already tired and discouraged from trying to teach the gospel to people who didn't want to hear about it. As he and his companion boarded the New York subway train, he looked around dejectedly at the people, seeing "them as hard, calloused, uncaring, and impossible to communicate with."

Elder Allen glanced up as a man dressed in rags entered the car. He was blind and carried a well-used saxophone with a tin cup hung on the front of it. The man placed the saxophone to his lips, and as he began to play, "a soft, delicate melody filled the air. In an almost imperceptible manner, the atmosphere of the car changed and the people quieted. . . . The sightless stranger reached out to touch every heart within hearing with a song played from his own heart. It lingered in the air, and a warm feeling ran through the discouraged missionary, waking up something that had been sleeping deep within him."

When the song ended, Elder Allen looked around and saw the same people differently than he had before. "A common warmth had melted the ice that before had stood between them all. Suddenly, every person wanted to give something to this ragged old man who had shared so much with them. . . . Each of them reached out to fill the blind man's tin cup with coins. They also whispered expressions of gratitude and encouragement. . . .

"Elder Allen looked across the car at his companion who met

his eyes with a knowing smile. He looked quickly down at the ground, ashamed of what he had felt a few short minutes before. 'The blind man knew long ago what I needed so badly to learn,' he thought. 'Everyone has a heart—it just takes a special song to touch those hearts.' " (See Richard B. Williams, *New Era*, August 1978, pp. 44–46.)

The author of this fictitious account taught, in a beautiful and sensitive way, the important truth that all of us are children of God and that our hearts can be touched if the song is right. One song that touches many hearts is the song of service. Sometimes we preach too early and too much instead of giving patient, loving service. Ammon, one of the sons of Mosiah, understood this principle well and used the song of service to reach the hearts of King Lamoni and many of his people.

When Ammon entered the land of Ishmael he was captured and taken before the king. The king could slay Ammon, throw him into prison, or cast him out of his land, according to his will and pleasure. When Ammon told the king that he desired to live among the Lamanites, maybe for the rest of his life, the king was pleased with him and asked him to marry one of his daughters. Ammon's response to the king's request eventually permitted the conversion of thousands of Lamanites: "But Ammon said unto him: Nay, but *I will be thy servant.* Therefore Ammon became a servant to king Lamoni. And it came to pass that he was set among other servants to watch the flocks of Lamoni, according to the custom of the Lamanites." (Alma 17:25, italics added.)

Ammon was not just a token servant—he put his whole heart into serving the king. In fact, King Lamoni later said, "Surely there has not been any servant among all my servants that has been so faithful as this man; for even he doth remember all my commandments to execute them" (Alma 18:10). Because of Ammon's faithful and powerful service, King Lamoni eventually asked him to teach him about his God.

Before pure testimony and the word of God can penetrate some hearts, those hearts have to be softened by service. Such was the case with one fourteen-year-old girl. She was headed down the wrong road in life until four girls touched her through numerous acts of service. Every week at least one of them would visit her for an hour or two and invite her to come to Mutual. When they saw her at school they always stopped and talked with her. They sat by her in the classes they had together and invited themselves over to her house to study with her. Two of these four girls were cheerleaders, and the other two were very popular, yet they showed a genuine interest in this girl.

When the girl had her next birthday her family did nothing to make it special, but the four girls did. When she later ended up in the hospital for three weeks she was visited every day by these girls, who brought her reading material, candy, and a radio, and they spent many hours talking and playing games together.

The clincher was the day she found out her mother had passed away. She left the house and started to run in the rain. She explains what happened next: "I ran until I was exhausted, but I did not stop. My face was swollen and my head hurt. Still I ran. Then, suddenly, I saw from the opposite direction someone coming toward me. I paused and wiped my eyes. Could it be? One of those four Mutual girls, the girls who truly cared about me. One of those girls was running through the rain for me. I began to run again and when we met I threw my arms around that girl and we both collapsed to the ground. I sat there crying, and she cried with me."

It is not surprising that when this young woman was married in the temple these four girls were in attendance. Talking about that special day, this young woman said: "I knelt across the altar from my sweetheart and in the reflection of mirrors were those four Mutual girls, standing, with tears running down their cheeks. They had made this possible for me.

"I'll never know why I had been so important to them. Me, a nobody. I can only thank my Father in heaven for those girls and pray with all my heart that there are many more like them in his Church." (See Blaine M. Yorgason and Brenton G. Yorgason, *Others* [Salt Lake City: Bookcraft, 1978], pp. 1–4.)

Many of us feel hesitant about discussing the gospel with nonmembers or with those who are less active in the Church, but all of us can look for opportunities to serve. As we share ourselves and our love, the time will come when these people will desire to know more about the Church. Then their hearts can be touched with testimony and with the word of God. But for many people the special song that will touch their hearts first is the song of service.

Chapter 36

WISE,
YET HARMLESS

ALMA 18:22

After King Lamoni had been told how Ammon had defended his flocks, he had many questions for Ammon. He wondered whether Ammon was the Great Spirit and by what power he "slew and smote off the arms" of those who scattered the sheep. He even told Ammon that he would give him anything he wanted if he would answer his questions. The book of Alma then relates: "Now Ammon being wise, yet harmless, he said unto Lamoni: Wilt thou hearken unto my words, if I tell thee by what power I do these things? And this is the thing that I desire of thee. And the king answered him, and said: Yea, I will believe all thy words." (Alma 18:22–23.)

This idea of Ammon's being "harmless" is an interesting one. He had just killed many Lamanites and wounded many more, yet he is referred to as harmless. Many times when we desire to teach others the gospel, we approach them in such a way that causes them to feel threatened or backed into a corner. They are afraid that they or their beliefs will be made to look foolish or that they will lose face in some way. This is especially true if family members or friends are present. Ammon's approach of service and love was totally nonthreatening to the king. Many a king would have been concerned about asking a servant for information, especially in front of many of his subjects, but Ammon was spiritually and emotionally harmless.

The Lord explained this approach to the latter-day Church:

"Let your preaching be the warning voice, every man to his neighbor, in mildness and in meekness" (D&C 38:41). He also declared: "Thou shalt declare glad tidings, yea, publish it upon the mountains, and upon every high place, and among every people that thou shalt be permitted to see. And thou shalt do it with all humility, trusting in me, reviling not against revilers." (D&C 19:29–30.)

When we argue about the scriptures or try to force our opinions upon others, we are following the promptings of Satan. The scriptures teach us that contention is of the devil, and arguing never has and never will convert someone to the Church.

This was demonstrated by two missionaries who, in the heat of battle, quoted a scripture that showed a man wrong and them right. The man claimed he would believe it if they could find it in his own Bible. When the missionaries turned to the passage in his Bible, he serenely ripped the page out and said, "See, that scripture is not in my Bible."

When we approach others in the spirit of meekness and mildness, the Holy Ghost can replace feelings of apprehension and contention with peace and understanding. This gospel approach came very naturally to Elder Parker, and he was very successful as a missionary. Elder Parker's zone leader called one morning and asked to accompany the Elder during his next "first discussion," so he could pick up some good ideas. Although Elder Parker felt that he did nothing special in his teaching, he said he would be glad to work with the zone leader.

The next day the zone leader received a phone call, and he joined Elder Parker in teaching the first discussion to a young family. Nothing impressive happened during the discussion. In fact, Elder Parker was less dynamic than most of the missionaries the zone leader had taught with. He was very humble and quiet, and the family had to listen very carefully just to hear what he was saying.

When the formal part of the discussion was over, Elder Parker leaned forward and put his hand on the father's arm. He looked him straight in the eyes and told him how much he loved him and his family. Elder Parker then bore one of the most humble and powerful testimonies that the zone leader had ever heard. By this time every member of the family, including the father, and both Elders had tears streaming down their cheeks.

Elder Parker then quietly and with great dignity taught the father how to pray. As the family and the Elders knelt together, the father prayed that they might receive testimonies of their own and thanked Heavenly Father for the great love that he felt. Two weeks later the whole family was baptized. The zone leader learned the great power of quiet humility, love, and testimony.

Because Ammon and Elder Parker used gospel approaches that were nonthreatening, people were more inclined to listen to them. This gave them an opportunity to share their great love and to bear their testimonies. We will enjoy much more success and happiness in our own lives as we learn to approach our friends in meekness and mildness.

Chapter 37

HE WAS ASTONISHED EXCEEDINGLY

ALMA 20:26–27

Jack had fought with his father throughout his life. When he was seventeen, after a serious argument, Jack told his father that he was leaving and would not be returning. As he packed his bags, his tearful mother pleaded with him to stay, but Jack refused to listen. Just as Jack was leaving the yard, his father called to him and said, "Jack, I know that a large share of the blame for your leaving rests with me. For this I am truly sorry. I want you to know that if you should ever wish to return home, you'll always be welcome. And I'll try to be a better father to you. I want you to know that I'll always love you."

Jack did not respond but went to the bus station and boarded a bus to a faraway city. As he sat on the bus the words "I love you," spoken by his father, kept going through his mind. He realized that he would never be happy until he went home and returned that love with love of his own.

Jack got off the bus at the next stop and purchased a return fare home. It was after midnight when he entered the house. "There in the rocking chair sat his father, his head in his hands. As he looked up and saw Jack, he rose from the chair and they rushed into each other's arms. Jack often said, 'Those last years that I was home were among the happiest of my life.' " (See Thomas S. Monson, *Ensign*, April 1987, pp. 5–6.)

Of all the powers of the universe there are few that are greater or more powerful than love. Love can overcome bitterness, hate, anger, and resentment, and it can replace them with peace, unity, and concern for one another. Other than the power of the Holy Ghost, love is by far the most important ingredient in the conversion of those around us to the gospel of Jesus Christ.

It was the great love of the sons of Mosiah that led to their marvelous success among the Lamanites. This love was demonstrated by Ammon when he first met the father of King Lamoni. Ammon's brothers had been cast into prison in the city of Middoni, and Ammon and Lamoni were on their way to release them when they met Lamoni's father, who was king over all of the Lamanites. This powerful king hated the Nephites and he commanded his son to kill Ammon and return to his city, but Lamoni refused. This angered the king even more, and he drew his sword to kill his own son. Ammon not only was concerned about Lamoni but did not want the king to lose his soul by shedding the innocent blood of his son.

After Ammon placed himself between Lamoni and his father to try to reason with him, the king attacked him in an effort to kill him. Ammon withstood his blows and wounded the king, who began to plead for his life. He even offered Ammon half his kingdom if he would spare his life, but Ammon asked only that Lamoni's life be spared and his brothers be released from prison.

When the king "saw that Ammon had no desire to destroy him, and when he also saw the great love he had for his son Lamoni, he was astonished exceedingly, and said: Because this is all that thou hast desired, that I would release thy brethren, and suffer that my son Lamoni should retain his kingdom, behold, I will grant unto you that my son may retain his kingdom from this time and forever; and I will govern him no more—and I will also grant unto thee that thy brethren may be cast out of prison, and thou and thy brethren may come unto me, in my kingdom; for I shall greatly desire to see thee. For the king was greatly astonished at the words which he had spoken, and also at the words which had been spoken by his son Lamoni, therefore he was desirous to learn them." (Alma 20:26–27.)

Because of the great love demonstrated by Ammon at this time, the king and many of his people accepted the gospel and were baptized into the Church. This great power that comes when we truly love everyone is also demonstrated in the following story:

In the course of the Armenian atrocities a young woman

and her brother were pursued down the street by a Turkish soldier, cornered in an angle of the wall, and the brother was slain before his sister's eyes. She dodged down an alley, leaped a wall, and escaped. Later, being a nurse, she was forced by the Turkish authorities to work in the military hospital. Into her ward was brought, one day, the same Turkish soldier who had slain her brother. He was very ill. A slight inattention would insure his death. The young woman, now safe in America, confesses to the bitter struggle that took place in her mind. The old Adam cried, "Vengeance"; the new Christ cried, "Love." And, equally to the man's good and to her own, the better side of her conquered, and she nursed him as carefully as any other patient in the ward. The recognition had been mutual and one day, unable longer to restrain his curiosity, the Turk asked his nurse why she had not let him die, and when she replied, "I am a follower of him who said 'Love your enemies and do them good,' " he was silent for a long time. At last he spoke: "I never knew that there was such a religion. If that is your religion tell me more about it, for I want it." (Harry Emerson Fosdick, *Twelve Tests of Character* [New York: Harper and Brothers, 1923], pp. 166–167.)

When God said that "charity never faileth," he was talking about this kind of love. It never fails because it is very difficult not to respond to those who love us, overlook our faults, and accept us as we are. It is easy to see why Jesus taught that love is by far the most important commandment and one that encompasses all of the other commandments. As we grow in our love for others, we will find ourselves much more effective in helping those we serve draw closer to God. We will also find greater enjoyment in our service, for love that is given away returns manyfold.

Chapter 38

SAVING
SOME SOUL

ALMA 26:30–37

In a revelation given through Joseph Smith, the Lord said, "Remember the worth of souls is great in the sight of God" (D&C 18:10). The great worth of each person may never have been expressed better than by a mother whose two-year-old baby was left severely handicapped after nearly drowning. Fourteen years later, after much pain and personal growth, she wrote the following entry in her journal:

> A few weeks ago I gave a seminar on identity and personal growth at a large gathering of young women. We met in a beautiful cabin at Sundance [ski resort]. Near the end, I was trying to develop the idea that we are not our achievements or our accumulation of possessions. Our worth is intrinsic, because we are children of our Heavenly Father. When we become competitive with each other in order to feel worthwhile, we damage our potential for loving relationships and the capacity to experience closeness with others.
>
> Quite spontaneously, I decided to use Daniel [her handicapped son] as an example to illustrate what I was trying to teach. Most of the young women know Daniel, by sight or from interacting with him. I asked the young women if he had any worth: he can't walk; he can't talk; he will never achieve worldly success. They vigorously agreed that he is a valuable

person. They love to be around him. He radiates love, caring, purity. His spirit shines forth as a blessing to others.

I believe those who were there experienced a vivid affirmation of what is really of worth in this life. There was a wonderful, loving spirit in that gathering of young women and leaders. There were tears as hearts were touched by the knowledge of their own value. (Marian S. Bergin, *Ensign*, August 1990, p. 21.)

Individual worth does not depend on occupation, intelligence, appearance, nationality, race, family name, or economic status. Every one of us is of great worth because each of us is a spirit child of God. Even our sins do not change our worth in God's sight. When this transcendent truth finally sinks deeply into our hearts, the concern we have for others blossoms and grows.

God has promised us great joy as we help others accept Christ and his atonement. After seeing thousands of Lamanites respond to the gospel Ammon shared the following feelings:

> And we have suffered all manner of afflictions, and all this, that *perhaps we might be the means of saving some soul*; and we supposed that our joy would be full if perhaps we could be the means of saving some.
>
> Now behold, we can look forth and see the fruits of our labors; and are they few? I say unto you, Nay, they are many; yea, and we can witness of their sincerity, because of their love towards their brethren and also towards us. . . .
>
> Now have we not reason to rejoice? Yea, I say unto you, there never were men that had so great reason to rejoice as we, since the world began. . . .
>
> Now my brethren, we see that God is mindful of every people, whatsoever land they may be in; yea, he numbereth his people, and his bowels of mercy are over all the earth. Now this is my joy, and my great thanksgiving; yea, and I will give thanks unto my God forever. Amen. (Alma 26:30–31, 35, 37, italics added.)

Notice that Ammon said they suffered all manner of afflictions before they were able to experience success and joy. Helping others come unto Christ is not always easy, but it is always rewarding.

Sister Jayne B. Malan, first counselor in the Young Women

General Presidency, had an experience when she was twelve that helped her understand how Christ feels about every soul. She lived on a ranch where one winter storm had left about 350 lambs without mothers to take care of them. The responsibility to feed these lambs fell upon the shoulders of the children. Many of the lambs were lost to coyotes or starvation. As hard as it was to find five to ten dead lambs every morning, she was almost devastated when she found her own pet lamb dead.

> One morning my lamb didn't come when I called. I found it later that day under the willows by the creek. It was dead. With tears streaming down my face, I picked up my lamb and went to find my father. Looking up at him, I said, "Dad, isn't there someone who can help us feed our lambs?"
>
> After a long moment he said, "Jayne, once a long, long time ago, someone else said almost those same words. He said, 'Feed my lambs. . . . Feed my sheep. . . . Feed my sheep.' " (John 21:15–17.) Dad put his arms around me and let me cry for a time, then went with me to bury my lamb.
>
> It wasn't until many years later that I fully realized the meaning of my father's words. I was pondering the scripture in Moses that says, "For behold, this is my work and my glory—to bring to pass the immortality and eternal life of [all mankind]." (Moses 1:39.) As I thought about the mission of the Savior, I remembered the summer of the lambs, and, for a few brief moments, I thought I could sense how the Savior must feel with so many lambs to feed, so many souls to save. And I knew in my heart that he needed my help. (*Ensign*, November 1989, pp. 78–79.)

God needs our help also in the important work of saving souls. By working as hard as they could, Sister Malan's family saved more than one hundred lambs that would have, otherwise, died. We can't touch everyone, but we can make a difference. There are many children of God who are lost only because they know not where to look for the truth. Others, through an outpouring of love and service on our part, will change their direction and come back to the fold. God cares about these "lost souls," and he will help us reach them if we will but put our hearts into the work.

Chapter 39

THE DEVIL WILL NOT SUPPORT HIS CHILDREN

ALMA 30:58–60

Korihor was one of several anti-Christs in the Book of Mormon. The devil appeared to him and told him to teach that there was no penalty for sin and no Christ. When Alma testified that there *was* a Christ, Korihor asked for a sign and was subsequently struck dumb. The people became convinced of his wickedness and were reconverted to the gospel of Christ.

As Mormon abridged this part of the record he told what happened next and then drew a conclusion that is important to all of us: "And Korihor did go about from house to house, begging food for his support. And it came to pass that as he went forth among the people . . . behold, he was run upon and trodden down, even until he was dead. And thus we see the end of him who perverteth the ways of the Lord; and thus we see that the devil will not support his children at the last day, but doth speedily drag them down to hell." (Alma 30:58–60.)

We receive our wages from whomever we "list to obey." Most of us have heard people say that they do not want to serve God—they just want to do their own thing. These people can serve themselves all of their lives, but when the day of judgment and reward comes they will be able to give themselves nothing, and they will receive nothing from God because they never served him. God has promised, to those who serve him, everything he has—including godhood, an eternal family, and the opportunity of eternal increase.

Some of Satan's rewards for service and loyalty to him are pain, suffering, depression, and unhappiness. Satan has no worthwhile reward to offer for obedience to him, and if he did, he wouldn't make it available to his followers. Elder Mark E. Petersen described how Satan feels about us: "Inasmuch as he himself now can never be exalted, he tries to prevent all others from achieving that goal. What does he care about us, except to destroy us? We are his targets, we are his prey. With lies and intrigue he would persuade us that happiness may be found in sin, that gain may be had through fraud, deception, licentiousness, and even murder. . . . With every conceivable device he wages war with the Saints, endeavoring to make them miserable like himself." (*The Way of the Master* [Salt Lake City: Bookcraft, 1974], pp. 3–4.)

A great comparison between the motives of God and the motives of Satan is found in the book of Moses. Enoch was shown a vision that included the people at the time of Noah. Notice Satan's feelings for these people who had loyally done the things he had prompted them to do: "And [Enoch] beheld Satan; and he had a great chain in his hand, and it veiled the whole face of the earth with darkness; and he looked up and laughed, and his angels rejoiced" (Moses 7:26).

When we realize that Satan was rejoicing at such things as child abuse, cruelty, murder, immorality, and all types of vulgarity and profanity, it intensifies our desire to avoid Satan and all he promulgates.

Enoch also recorded the way God felt about the people at Noah's time: "And it came to pass that the God of heaven looked upon the residue of the people, and *he wept*; and Enoch bore record of it, saying: How is it that the heavens weep, and shed forth their tears as the rain upon the mountains?"

God's response included the following: "I can stretch forth mine hands and hold all the creations which I have made; and mine eye can pierce them also, and among all the workmanship of mine hands there has not been so great wickedness as among thy brethren. But behold, their sins shall be upon the heads of their fathers; Satan shall be their father, and misery shall be their doom; and the whole heavens shall weep over them, even all the workmanship of mine hands; wherefore should not the heavens weep, seeing these shall suffer?" (Moses 7:28, 36–37, italics added.)

A bishop recently saw the fruits of following Satan and of following God illustrated in the life of a sister in his ward. When she came to see him she had committed a serious offense against God. In fact, it was so hideous to her that she had blocked part of it out of her conscious mind. As she sat in his office and began to tell why she was there, she suddenly realized, fully, the abhorrent crime she had committed. The bishop watched her face become filled with intense pain and shame as the realization of what she had done finally came to her.

She struggled with self-hate and depression for several years before she allowed God to finally enter into her heart. Today she is happy and productive because of the great miracle of repentance and the profound gift of the Atonement.

Alma the Younger described these same feelings: "Nevertheless, after wading through much tribulation, repenting nigh unto death, the Lord in mercy hath seen fit to snatch me out of an everlasting burning, and I am born of God. My soul hath been redeemed from the gall of bitterness and bonds of iniquity. I was in the darkest abyss; but now I behold the marvelous light of God. My soul was racked with eternal torment; but I am snatched, and my soul is pained no more." (Mosiah 27:28–29.)

As we think about the animosity and hatred of Satan, and of the great love and mercy of God, it seems foolish to even consider doing anything but what God wants us to do. When we consider the wages each has to offer, the choice becomes even easier to make. Only the very foolish would desire what Satan has to offer over the great blessings that come through obedience to God.

Chapter 40

NEVER SPEAKING
OF GOD AGAIN

ALMA 31:23

Sometimes we forget the purpose of our Sunday meetings and allow them to become the very center of our religion and worship. Sitting in a meeting doesn't make us Christians any more than sitting in a library makes us scholars or holding a violin makes us musicians. One of the most insightful definitions of the purpose of churches was written by C. S. Lewis:

> It is easy to think that the Church has a lot of different objects—education, building, missions, holding services. Just as it is easy to think the State has a lot of different objects—military, political, economic, and what not. But in a way things are much simpler than that. The State exists simply to promote and to protect the ordinary happiness of human beings in this life. A husband and wife chatting over a fire, a couple of friends having a game of darts in a pub, a man reading a book in his own room or digging in his own garden—that is what the State is there for. And unless they are helping to increase and prolong and protect such moments, all the laws, parliaments, armies, courts, police, economics, etc., are simply a waste of time. In the same way the Church exists for nothing else but to draw men into Christ, to make them little Christs. If they are not doing that, all the cathedrals, clergy, missions, sermons, even the Bible itself, are simply a waste of time. (C. S. Lewis, *Mere Christianity* [New York: Macmillan, 1960], pp. 169–70.)

Meetings are for showing our devotion to our Father in Heaven and for learning and planning how to better live the gospel and make it available to others. The purpose of this life is to become more like God, not to attend a certain number of meetings.

The Zoramites had completely lost the purpose of Sabbath worship and, in fact, the whole purpose of worship. They would, one at a time, give the same prayer from a stand in the middle of their synagogue, and "after the people had all offered up thanks after this manner, they returned to their homes, never speaking of their God again until they had assembled themselves together again to the holy stand, to offer up thanks after their manner" (Alma 31:23).

Religion is much more than just Sunday worship. It is a complete way of life. We ought to be as excited about our membership in the Church as a young girl named Marsha was. When her family moved to Downey, California, she climbed up on the back fence and yelled to the neighbors that she could see, "Hey, you people down there; hey, all of you people down there! Hey, you people! We're Mormons!" (See Paul H. Dunn, *BYU Speeches of the Year*, October 19, 1971, p. 9.)

The Lord has told us that if we are going to overcome sin and become more like him, we need to not only keep the Sabbath day holy but also offer up our vows "on all days and at all times" (see D&C 59:9–11). Becoming a celestial person is not a three-hour-a-week job or a one-day-a-week job, but a full-time job. Sometimes we hesitate to live our religion because of what others may think or say. This not only slows down our own spiritual growth but hurts the growth of those around us as well.

President N. Eldon Tanner described an experience that is relevant here. Two or three related families were camping together and decided to hold a family home evening during which, according to President Tanner, the following took place:

> One boy said, "What should you do when you are out with young fellows camping or with a group out away from home fishing or anything of the kind, and when you go to bed you want to pray?"
>
> Someone suggested, "Well, you might go outside and pray, outside the tent. Or if you're in a home, or a building where there is a bathroom, you might go in the bathroom and pray."
>
> Another one said, "Well, couldn't you go to bed and pray?"

One of the girls of the same age spoke up and said, "Why can't you pray where they are?" She said, "I have been out with a group of girls, and I have prayed with those girls there. All the girls pray, at least they did when I was with them. They knelt down and prayed when I did." (*Improvement Era*, December 1964, p. 1084.)

As we continue to live the gospel under all circumstances, we will develop celestial traits and become more and more godlike. As this happens we will be fulfilling our purpose for being here upon the earth. Since the process of becoming like God does not take place on a part-time basis, we need to consistently apply, each and every day, gospel principles such as love, kindness, and unselfishness. As we do this we become more loving, kind, and unselfish, and therefore more like our Father in Heaven.

Chapter 41

DESIRE TO BELIEVE

ALMA 32:27

What if a person being taught by the missionaries doesn't even believe in God? Since he has no faith, how can he get an answer to a prayer? The answer to this question was given by Alma: "But behold, if ye will awake and arouse your faculties, even to an experiment upon my words, and exercise a particle of faith, yea, even if ye can no more than desire to believe, let this desire work in you, even until ye believe in a manner that ye can give place for a portion of my words" (Alma 32:27).

It is important to notice that Alma did not say that a person must desire to find out whether some teaching is true, but that one must *desire to believe* that it is true. The beginning of faith is when we hear some truth such as "There is a living prophet on the earth today," or "You can be together with your family for eternity," and we say to ourselves, "Oh, I hope that is true—that would be such a wonderful thing." This is when the truth begins to swell within our breasts and our faith begins to grow (see Alma 32:28–30).

The importance of desiring to know it is true was well illustrated by a man who accepted a Book of Mormon from two missionaries. They promised him that if he would read it with a sincere heart and ask God in humble prayer, he would know the truthfulness of the book. When the missionaries returned he handed them the book and said that, by using their formula, he had proven the Book of Mormon false. When they asked him how he had accomplished this feat he indicated that he had read several pages of the

Book of Mormon, knelt down, and asked God to strike him dead if the book was true. Since he was still living, the book had to be false. This man never desired to believe, only to show that the book was false.

Once a person hears the truth and desires to believe, the next step is to nourish the word with great care (see Alma 32:37). The more we desire to believe, the more nourishment we will give the word. When I was a missionary my companion and I met a man who claimed that he was seriously investigating the truthfulness of the Church. After prayerfully reading the Book of Mormon every day for two weeks, he said that he had received no indication of its truthfulness. We asked him at what time of day he did his studying and praying, and we encouraged him to continue. We then planned our schedule for the next day so that we could drop in on him unannounced, shortly after his study time.

Much to our surprise, when we arrived he was reading through a pile of pornographic magazines. When we asked him about his Book of Mormon study we found that he had interrupted his magazine study long enough to read ten minutes in the Book of Mormon. As our discussion with this man continued it soon became apparent that his desire for and nourishment of the word left something to be desired.

Thousands of other people, however, have put Alma's experiment to the test with positive results. As a matter of fact, every person who has ever carried out his experiment as specified has received a testimony of the word. If we want to look for secular parallels, we can say that Alma's experiment is like that of a scientist. When a scientist exactly follows a set procedure he gets the same results as other scientists get. When a mother follows a recipe perfectly she receives what the recipe promised. When we follow Alma's inspired process not only do we receive increased faith but also we eventually receive a precious fruit which "is sweet above all that is sweet, and which is white above all that is white, yea, and pure above all that is pure," which is the fruit of "everlasting life" (see Alma 32:41–42).

Chapter 42

DO NOT PROCRASTINATE
UNTIL THE END

ALMA 34:31–33

A young man who was involved in pilot training had never learned to keep the rules or to listen to those who knew more than he did. When he should have been studying emergency procedures, in case he ever had to bail out of a plane, he could be found on the golf course or in the swimming pool. He would talk someone into marking him present so he would not have to undergo the emergency training. When he was asked what he was going to do in an emergency he indicated that there wasn't going to be one.

A few months later his plane caught on fire and he died in the crash. The pilot who was with him, who had prepared himself, escaped from the plane. (See Robert D. Hales, *Ensign*, May 1990, pp. 39–40.)

The gospel training we receive as we study, pray, and obey God's commandments prepares us for the many emergencies we will face in our lives—including the big one when we stand before God to be judged. If we follow the Lord's handbook of instructions (the standard works) and listen to and obey our instructors (our leaders and the Holy Ghost), when we are faced with difficult problems or decisions we will be prepared.

The problem is that many of us tend to put off our training until a later time. Satan knows he can't just get us to say we won't live the gospel, so he instead gets us to say that we will start living it tomorrow instead of today. We will do our home teaching next week. As soon as the children are older we will start studying the scriptures daily. Family Home Evening will become part of our schedule as soon as summer is over and school has started. Our plans are made; our intentions are honorable; the future will surely be ours.

Amulek warned us about the seriousness of procrastination:

> Yea, I would that ye would come forth and harden not your hearts any longer; for behold, now is the time and the day of your salvation; and therefore, if ye will repent and harden not your hearts, immediately shall the great plan of redemption be brought about unto you.
>
> For behold, this life is the time for men to prepare to meet God; yea, behold the day of this life is the day for men to perform their labors.
>
> And now, as I said unto you before, as ye have had so many witnesses, therefore, I beseech of you that ye do not procrastinate the day of your repentance until the end; for after this day of life, which is given us to prepare for eternity, behold, if we do not improve our time while in this life, then cometh the night of darkness wherein there can be no labor performed. (Alma 34:31–33.)

Procrastination affects not only our next life but also our happiness and success in this life. Procrastination slows down our own spiritual growth and the growth of the kingdom. Those who home teach or who visit teach on the last day of the month are less effective because those they visit may question their love and true motives. Church lessons prepared just before they are given are usually hurried and often lack the insight and inspiration that can come as a lesson is thought about for a week or two. Late reports require extra calls to be made, wasting time on both the ward and the stake level, and because of the rush involved they may be less accurate. Worry, friction, contention, and lessened quality and effectiveness are common fruits of procrastination.

I read a story many years ago about a teenage girl who had a fight with her younger brother and decided to teach him a lesson by refusing to forgive him. The next morning as she left for school she saw the sadness in his eyes, and she thought to herself that she would make it up to him later.

That was the last time she saw her brother alive. That afternoon as he raced across the street on his bike, he was hit and killed by a car. As the days went by this girl remembered the many kind things her brother had done for her, and over and over again she found herself saying, "If only! If only I could do it again! If only I had one more chance!"

There are probably no sadder words than *if only*. When we decide to stop procrastinating and to start doing the things we should do when they should be done, we quickly replace the words *if only* with the words *thank goodness*. I heard one young man talk about the death of his brother and he said, "Thank goodness our last moments together were happy ones in which we expressed our love for one another." When judgment day comes I can see us saying, "Thank goodness we were sealed as a family and kept our covenants," or "Thank goodness we repented of our sins and didn't wait until it was too late," or "Thank goodness we put the Lord first in our lives and kept his commandments," or "Thank goodness we introduced the gospel to the Redfords and they can be here with us."

Chapter 43

HE WILL FULFIL
HIS PROMISES

ALMA 37:16–17

Junius had received an unusual promise in his patriarchal blessing. He had been told that he would not leave this life until he wanted to. Since Junius loved life, he was still going strong when he reached eighty years old. He missed his wife, but he had told several friends and relatives that he wanted to live long enough to see a grandchild go on a mission and to have great-grandchildren. Eventually great-grandchildren were born, and a year or two later one of his grandsons accepted a mission call.

Junius was very excited when he was asked to speak at the farewell, and the grandson felt grateful to be able to have his grandfather participate on the program. Three days after his grandson left for the mission field Junius was rushed to the hospital with serious health problems, and both of his legs were amputated. The doctor attending Junuis was an old friend, and as they visited, Junius mentioned to him that he felt it was time for him to die. He told him how much he missed his wife and looked forward to being able to be with her again. He indicated that with his grandson leaving on his mission all of his earthly desires had been fulfilled. A few hours later Junius left this life and entered the spirit world to what must have been a glorious reunion with his sweetheart. The Lord's promise, made more than sixty years before, had been fulfilled.

This is not surprising, since every promise that God ever makes will be fulfilled if we do our part. Alma promised his son Helaman that "God is powerful to the fulfilling of all his words. For he will fulfil all his promises which he shall make unto you, for he has fulfilled his promises which he has made unto our fathers." (Alma 37:16–17.) In the latter days the Lord said, "What I the Lord have spoken, I have spoken, and I excuse not myself; and though the heavens and the earth pass away, my word shall not pass away, but shall all be fulfilled" (D&C 1:38).

In a world of broken promises and shifting loyalties it brings great peace and comfort to be able to have total confidence in the Lord. If we marry in the temple and keep our covenants we will be sealed for eternity. When we repent by turning our whole heart and soul toward God, we are forgiven of our sins and they are remembered no more (see D&C 58:42). As we study and pray about the Book of Mormon with real intent, our prayers are answered and a testimony is received.

One of the greatest promises God has given us is that, because of his love for us, he will respond to the righteous desires of our hearts. A man named Carl, who had been a faithful servant of God all of his life, was a recipient of this great promise. While Carl was serving a mission he received a letter telling of a serious accident that involved some of his friends. While they had been on an Aaronic Priesthood outing the huge truck carrying the boys and their equipment had slipped over a cliff, and many of the boys had been killed or seriously injured.

The letter said that one of the boys, whose jaw had been broken, had been asked to sing at the funeral of some of the boys who had been killed. At first, because his jaw was completely wired shut the boy had said no. But as he came to realize how much it would mean to the parents of the dead boys, he reconsidered. He was promised that if he would place his trust in the Lord, he would be able to sing.

Just before the funeral the wires were removed from his jaw. As he got up to sing the congregation waited in quiet anticipation to see what would happen. The Lord performed a miracle that morning, and the boy sang better and sweeter than he had ever sung before. His music brought great peace and comfort in a time of real need.

As Carl read about this inspiring event he knelt down, with tears streaming down his cheeks, and he asked God for a miracle of his own. He told God how much it would mean to him to hear his friend sing that song. As he got up from his knees he felt that God had heard his prayer and would answer it somehow.

As the years passed by Carl almost forgot about this request, but God didn't. One day, many years later, a seminary student of Carl's brought an audiotape to use for a devotional. She told the class the story about the accident that had happened long before and about the miracle the Lord had performed during the funeral. She then said that her mother had been present and had taped the boy who sang with the blessing and power of God. As Carl listened to this song from the past, his eyes filled with tears, and his heart filled with gratitude, and the Spirit whispered to him that this was the answer to the humble prayer he had offered many years before.

Because the answer to Carl's prayer was not vital to his physical or spiritual welfare, it demonstrates the great love that God has for each of us. As we fulfill our part of the covenants we have made with him, he not only will keep his promises but will bless us in all areas of our lives.

BRIDLE ALL
YOUR PASSIONS

ALMA 38:12

The most common form of bondage is not physical but spiritual in nature. President Spencer W. Kimball once described this type of bondage by using an analogy. When he was a boy he had the responsibility of caring for a vicious bull. Whenever the bull decided to attack, President Kimball would simply jerk the chain attached to a ring in the bull's nose, and the bull would become obedient and submissive. The bull could be completely controlled through the ring in his nose.

President Kimball likened the bull's situation to the way in which sin can control people's lives: "So does sin, as a ring in the nose, have the sinner under subjection. So is sin like handcuffs on the wrists, a ring in the nose, and slave bands around the neck. . . . What is needed is self-discipline. Can we imagine the angels or the gods not being in control of themselves in any particular? The question is of course ludicrous. Equally ridiculous is the idea that any of us can rise to the eternal heights without disciplining ourselves." (*The Miracle of Forgiveness* [Salt Lake City: Bookcraft, 1969], pp. 27–28.)

The very heart and soul of the gospel is love—the unselfish, unconditional love that the scriptures call charity. Christ taught that to love God and our fellowmen encompasses all of the other commandments. The importance of self-control and self-restraint in the development of this love was taught by Alma when he gave the following advice to Shiblon: "Use boldness, but not overbearance; and also see that ye bridle all your passions, that ye may be filled with love" (Alma 38:12).

Some learned men in today's world teach that it is important to find a way to release passions such as anger and lust—otherwise they will build up inside of us and cause us emotional damage. These people teach that the way to get rid of these feelings is to express them. Actually just the opposite seems to be true. When we give in to passions such as anger and lust they grow in intensity and become even more powerful in our lives. These and other passions decrease in power and control over our lives only through self-restraint and personal discipline.

The uncontrolled liberation of one passion soon leads to the release of other unwanted passions in our lives. This destructive process was described by President Spencer W. Kimball: "Once the carnal in man is no longer checked . . . there comes an avalanche of appetites which gathers momentum that is truly frightening. As one jars loose and begins to roll down hill, still another breaks loose, whether it is an increase in homosexuality, corruption, drugs, or abortion. Each began as an appetite that needed to be checked but which went unchecked." (*Ensign*, May 1978, p. 78.)

If left unchecked, passions such as anger, greed, hate, jealousy, lust, and pride can destroy feelings of love and unselfishness and seriously restrict the help that we receive from the Holy Ghost.

One man couldn't understand why he was constantly yelling at his wife and children and why he lacked the control he had previously enjoyed. Then he began to notice a correlation between his anger and another problem he had allowed to grow unrestrained—that of lust. The more he read and looked at materials that fed his lust, the more anger and impatience he showed toward others and the less love he was able to feel and display. As he finally restrained himself and overcame his lust, his feelings of anger and contention decreased and his love increased.

This man found that he had allowed his passions to grow until he could not overcome them by himself. Only through the combination of intense personal effort and the strength that he received from the Lord through constant and serious prayer was this man able to become free from the passions that were controlling his life and destroying his future. Just as the Lord helped this man, he will assist all of us in overcoming and subduing our passions and in nurturing and expanding our love for God and for all those we come in contact with.

Chapter 45

ALL THINGS SHALL BE RESTORED

ALMA 40:23

Sandee was a junior in high school when she read one of the Church's advertisements in the *Reader's Digest*. She called the toll-free number, and a copy of the Book of Mormon was sent to her. For the next few months she kept the book by her bed and read "bits and pieces" of it. Then she had an experience that eventually led to her seeking out and joining the Church: "One evening, as I was reading the passages in the book of Mosiah that explained death and resurrection, my understanding blossomed. I was overcome by a feeling of hope and promise. The following morning, I awoke to the news that my father had died. After a few moments of grieving, I felt my heart fill with a quiet peace. I knew that the promises in Mosiah about the resurrection were true." (Sandee Gladden West, *Ensign*, August 1990, pp. 48–49.)

The atonement of Jesus Christ breaks the bands of both spiritual and physical death. Most of our gratitude seems to be directed toward our opportunity to repent of our sins and overcome spiritual death. It seems that since the resurrection is a free gift to everyone, it is sometimes taken for granted and not appreciated as much as it could be. The resurrection is just as important to our exaltation as are repentance and the forgiveness of sins. Jacob emphasized the importance of the resurrection when he declared: "If the flesh should rise no more our spirits must become subject to that angel who fell from before the presence of the Eternal God, and became the devil, to rise no more. And our spirits must have become like unto him, and we become devils, angels to a devil, to be shut out from the presence of our God, and to remain with the father of lies, in misery, like unto himself." (2 Nephi 9:8–9.)

The quality of the resurrection is important also. It wouldn't be much fun to be resurrected with all of our physical ailments and sicknesses. Trying to keep our weight down during the few years that we live on the earth is disheartening enough—imagine trying to fight the battle of the bulge for all eternity! For those of us who have misplaced much of our hair somewhere along the path of life, just getting our hair back is something to look forward to.

It doesn't take much earnest reflection to realize that few blessings we will ever receive can match the blessing of being able to leave all of our mental and physical disabilities behind us and receive a perfect body. Alma promised us that "the soul shall be restored to the body, and the body to the soul; yea, and every limb and joint shall be restored to its body; yea, even a hair of the head shall not be lost; but all things shall be restored to their proper and perfect frame" (Alma 40:23).

I never really appreciated the great gift of the resurrection until my own mother died. She had received one of those bodies that don't work very well, and had suffered physical problems from the time she was young. More than twenty-five times she had found herself in the hospital for one major problem or another. During the last ten years of her life she had been bedridden and in constant pain. However, this did not keep her from serving others or from worshiping the Lord. She taught Primary from a bed in the living room and spent many hours knitting gifts for friends and family members. The phone became a vehicle of good works that she used to contact groups that advertised for volunteers and to call lists of lonely people. She filled fruit jars, prepared dinner, and tried to do as many things as possible, even though she was in constant traction and lay flat on her back in bed.

My mother tried to keep the Sabbath day holy. She would listen to Church tapes, read the scriptures, and make gifts to be given as a symbol of her love. Her courage and her devotion to God were a great inspiration to family members and all those who came in contact with her.

Finally her body had suffered enough pain and just quit working. The last few hours of her life were spent where she had been so many times before, in the hospital. Her family was gathered around her as her spirit quietly left her body. Since I was the oldest son, my father asked me to offer a family prayer. As the family members knelt to pray, the Spirit of the Lord filled that small hospital room—and the hearts of each of us—to overflowing. I found the Spirit directing my thoughts and my words as I thanked Heavenly Father for the great gift of the resurrection. For the first time in my life I realized what the resurrection was all about. My mother was finally going to receive a body without pain and without blemish. She was going to walk again and run again and do all of the physical and mental things that she had been restricted from doing. Tears flowed down my cheeks as I offered the family prayer, and tears still stain my cheeks as I think of my mother's coming resurrection day. I pray that all of us will feel eternally grateful to the Savior for the transcendent gift of the resurrection.

Chapter 46

WICKEDNESS NEVER WAS HAPPINESS

ALMA 41:10–11

The goal of every person is happiness. Most of our choices are made with this end in mind. Many people look forward to some event that is going to bring happiness into their lives. Teenagers are sure their sixteenth birthday will bring great happiness because they will be able to drive and date. Other young people feel they will be happy when they graduate from high school. When graduation arrives and they are still unhappy, they look forward to college graduation or to their marriage day as their next possibilities for happiness. Some adults can be heard to say that they think happiness will come when the baby is toilet trained or when they get a raise or pay off the mortgage. Some even look into the distant future and know that happiness will be part of their lives when they reach retirement age and can relax and see the world. Actually, none of these events will bring much lasting happiness by themselves.

Most of us have come to realize that happiness is a product of the choices we make each day. If we are not happy today, chances are we will not be happy tomorrow, or next week, or next year, unless we change what we are doing. In Psalm 118:24 we read, "This is the day which the Lord hath made; we will rejoice and be glad in it."

Happiness comes from living the word of God. It comes from service and unselfishness and pure love. It is the sweet and natural fruit of correct choices. Alma taught his son Corianton the source of both happiness and misery when he declared: "Do not suppose, because it has been spoken concerning restoration, that ye shall be restored from sin to happiness. Behold, I say unto you, wickedness never was happiness. And now, my son, all men that are in a state of nature, or I would say, in a carnal state, are in the gall of bitterness and in the bonds of iniquity; they are without God in the world, and they have gone contrary to the nature of God; therefore, they are in a state contrary to the nature of happiness." (Alma 41:10–11.)

Samuel, the great Lamanite prophet, warned the Nephites living in the city of Zarahemla that their destruction was made sure because they had "sought for happiness in doing iniquity, which thing is contrary to the nature of that righteousness which is in our great and Eternal Head" (Helaman 13:38).

People invite into their lives drugs, dishonesty, immorality, abortion, and all types of crude and offensive entertainment in their quest for happiness. Yet we have only to look around us to see that these things lead to heartache and misery. Some of these activities bring momentary pleasure that is sometimes mistaken for happiness, but this quickly wears off and discouragement and depression return.

That happiness really is the fruit of righteousness was well depicted in the change that took place in the life of a lady we will call Mary. When Mary was first contacted on her doorstep by the missionaries she was full of hate, resentment, and depression. Her husband had left her; her boys, ages eight and ten, had been kicked out of school for continued stealing; and her only means of financial support was a small government check. Besides these problems Mary had several severe health problems stemming from attempts she had made on her life.

She had tried to kill herself on three different occasions and had been declared "dead on arrival" at the hospital after two of those attempts. As she cursed the doctors who had restored her to life, the missionaries realized they were probably talking to the most unhappy person they had ever met.

Much to their amazement, Mary invited them to return, and even more to their astonishment, she became a "golden investigator." Within just a few weeks she had read the Book of Mormon, attended church several times, received a strong spiritual witness, and been baptized into the kingdom of God.

Even more remarkable was the metamorphosis that took place in her life as the gospel of Jesus Christ lifted her out of the gutter of depression and hopelessness into a world of faith and hope and beauty. She partook of the fruit of the tree of life and found it delicious. She became a truly happy person.

These wonderful happenings were followed by another surprising turn of events. Mary's husband, upon returning home for a brief visit and to pick up any loose cash he could find, noticed the great change in his wife and sons, and he investigated the Church for himself. Soon he too joined the Church, and a splintered family became whole again.

We will have our bad days and be faced with adversity and affliction, but as we do our best to live the gospel and give our hearts to God, he will fill our hearts with peace and joy. Joseph Smith said: "Happiness is the object and design of our existence; and will be the end thereof, if we pursue the path that leads to it; and this path is virtue, uprightness, faithfulness, holiness, and keeping all the commandments of God. . . . In obedience there is joy and peace unspotted." (*Teachings of the Prophet Joseph Smith* [Salt Lake City: Deseret Book Co., 1938], pp. 255–56.)

There is perhaps one warning that should be given. Some members of the Church "look beyond the mark" and make gospel living much harder than it really is. They feel that they have to be perfect in every way, and they constantly feel guilty because they are not doing everything to perfection. The Lord said, "Do not run faster or labor more than you have strength . . . but be diligent unto the end" (D&C 10:4). The direction we are traveling is more important than the speed we are going, and our motives and effort are far more important than precision and flawlessness. The Lord asks of us only our best, and our best is always good enough for him.

SHALL RETURN
TO YOU AGAIN

ALMA 41:14–15

Some years ago while Elder Hartman Rector, Jr., was away from home serving in the navy, a wealthy farmer who lived in his neighborhood passed away. When Elder Rector returned home he wondered about the size of the dead farmer's estate and asked his cousin, "How much did he leave?" His cousin answered, "He left it all; he didn't take any of it with him." (See *Ensign*, June 1971, p. 79.)

In terms of physical possessions, all of us are like this farmer— we leave them *all* behind. There are some things, however, that we can take with us when we leave this life. Alma mentioned some of these things to his son Corianton: "Therefore, my son, see that you are merciful unto your brethren; deal justly, judge righteously, and do good continually; and if ye do all these things then shall ye receive your reward; yea, ye shall have mercy restored unto you again; ye shall have justice restored unto you again; ye shall have a righteous judgment restored unto you again; and ye shall have good rewarded unto you again. For that which ye do send out *shall return unto you again,* and be restored; therefore, the word restoration more fully condemneth the sinner, and justifieth him not at all." (Alma 41:14–15, italics added.)

Alma also explained that "whosoever will come may come and partake of the waters of life freely; and whosoever will not come the same is not compelled to come; but in the last day it shall be restored unto him according to his deeds" (Alma 42:27).

When we leave this life we take with us what we are. If we have thought celestial thoughts and done celestial deeds and, therefore, become celestial in nature, we will inherit the celestial kingdom. But if we have sought to do evil, and therefore have become evil in nature, "and [have] not repented in [our] days, behold, evil shall be done unto [us], according to the restoration of God" (Alma 42:28).

One man who must have received a warm and glorious welcome when he passed through the veil was Elder A. Theodore Tuttle. His life was filled with kindness, generosity, and service to God and man. When he became very ill President Gordon B. Hinckley and President Ezra Taft Benson asked the membership of the Church to plead with Heavenly Father that he might be healed. In spite of the many faithful prayers that were offered in his behalf, he did not recover but died seven weeks later.

Shortly before Elder Tuttle's death, Elder Boyd K. Packer spent an afternoon with him as he reviewed his life and the many blessings that he had received from the Lord. These two men had been close friends much of their lives, and during the course of their conversation this humble, devoted servant of God told Elder Packer the following: "I talked to the Lord about those prayers for my recovery. I asked if the blessings were mine to do with as I pleased. If that could be so, I told the Lord that I wanted him to take them back from me and give them to those who needed them more. I begged the Lord to take back those blessings and give them to others."

Talking about this magnificent display of love, Elder Packer said, "Can you not believe that the Lord may have favored the pleadings of this saintly man above our own appeal for his recovery?" (*Ensign*, May 1987, p. 25.)

This principle that we receive what we send out applies most of the time, not only in the next life but in this life as well. Kindness begets kindness, and love given freely comes back to us again. When we treat our children with love, consideration, and respect, they desire to reciprocate these feelings. If we try to rule with anger and force, we receive in return contention and disrespect.

One sister, named Sister Miske, had an experience that helps us see how blessings given can be quickly returned:

> One wintry morning the Miskes were awakened by their
> neighbors. The neighbors, sixteen elderly patients from a

nearby nursing home, were without water because their water pump had broken. The Miskes shared their well water all day— until the well went dry that evening. Sister Miske then purchased eighteen one-gallon containers of purified water and called on other LDS neighbors to help. They gathered sixteen five-gallon jugs and filled them at the local meetinghouse. Three sisters did the patients' necessary laundry; one sister spent nine hours washing and drying sheets.

For three days, Sister Miske transported more than a ton of water in snowy weather, with temperatures often hovering around zero. After three and a half days, a new pump was installed at the nursing home, and things there returned to normal.

But things were not normal for the Miske family; their own well remained dry. Members of the nursing home's staff were more than happy to help the Miskes. The nursing home provided the family with water until spring, when the well began to flow again. (*Ensign*, September 1990, p. 31.)

This gospel principle is sometimes referred to as the law of the harvest—that whatsoever we sow we will also reap. If we desire friends, we need only to plant seeds of friendship. When we share our personal feelings with our children they tend to share their feelings with us. The thoughts, words, and deeds that we sow each day of our lives sprout and grow and return to us again. By planting seeds of love and kindness and unselfishness we are rewarded with fruit that is sweet and nourishing both here and in the world to come.

Chapter 48

COMPELLED RELUCTANTLY
TO CONTEND

ALMA 43–62

During World War II a German Latter-day Saint soldier was seriously wounded by an American bullet. "He told his leader, 'Please take a white flag and go to the other side and see if there is a Mormon elder who could administer to me.' What a bizarre request in a war of two mortal enemies. But seeing his condition, and anxious to satisfy what appeared to be a last request, the leader took the white flag, went across the enemy line, and asked for a Mormon elder. One was found and he, with the German, crossed the enemy line, laid his hands upon that brother's head, and commanded in the name of the Lord that he remain alive until help could be had." (James M. Paramore, *Ensign*, May 1983, p. 28.)

Throughout the teachings of Christ we find the great message that we should never hate someone who considers us his enemy, because we are all brothers and sisters. Even the Germans and Americans who were *not* members of the Church were children of God and members of the same spiritual family. If we are called by our country to participate in war, the gospel principles still apply. Perhaps so many chapters about war were included in the Book of Mormon because we live in a world filled with war and conflict.

At no time in the Book of Mormon were the righteous armies the aggressors, nor did they make preemptive attacks against an enemy that was obviously about to launch a war. They never waged wars where any issue but immediate survival was at stake, and they never killed or mistreated prisoners. At times every citizen was required to fight, while at other times honor and protection were given to pacifists. Much direction and insight concerning acceptable reasons for war and proper attitudes concerning war are given in the book of Alma.

The Amalekites were of a more wicked and murderous disposition than the Lamanites, and they wanted the Lamanites to go to war for personal reasons. "Now this [the Amalekite leader] did that he might preserve their hatred towards the Nephites, that he might bring them into subjection to the accomplishment of his designs. For behold, his designs were to stir up the Lamanites to anger against the Nephites; this he did that he might usurp great power over them, and also that he might gain power over the Nephites by bringing them into bondage." (Alma 43:7–8.)

These verses teach us that when we are filled with anger and hatred we can be easily manipulated by others and that hate and anger are never acceptable reasons for war. Any attempt at restoring peace would be effectively blocked so long as these feelings are present.

Some of the justifiable reasons for fighting a war are given in the following verse: "And now the design of the Nephites was to support their lands, and their houses, and their wives, and their children, that they might preserve them from the hands of their enemies; and also that they might preserve their rights and their privileges, yea, and also their liberty, that they might worship God according to their desires" (Alma 43:9).

God will justify our going to war if we do it to protect ourselves and our families, our homes and our property, and our freedom. Even if war is justified, our personal feelings are still important. The following scriptures clarify some of the attitudes that we should have concerning war and bloodshed:

> But, as I have said, in the latter end of the nineteenth year, yea, notwithstanding their peace amongst themselves, they were *compelled reluctantly* to contend with their brethren, the Lamanites.
>
> Yea, and in fine, their wars never did cease for the space of many years with the Lamanites, notwithstanding *their much reluctance*.
>
> Now, they were *sorry* to take up arms against the Laman-

ites, because *they did not delight in the shedding of blood*; yea, and
this was not all—they were sorry to be the means of sending so
many of their brethren out of this world into an eternal world,
unprepared to meet their God. (Alma 48:21–23, italics added.)

The Lord can bless us when we have no desire for gain or
power but only for defense. Because the Nephites were reluctant to
go to war, the Lord was on their side. Whether or not killing someone during a war is murder depends on what we desire in our
heart. If we are bloodthirsty and enjoy killing, we are held accountable, but if, like the Nephites, we abhor the shedding of blood
and desire to stop the bloodshed as soon as possible, we will not be
held responsible. Notice that the Nephites continued to refer to the
Lamanites as "their brethren" and even felt sorry for them because
they were being sent back to God unprepared.

Another important principle the book of Alma teaches us
about war is that righteousness and faith are more important than
missiles or the size of the army. Captain Moroni declared: "But
now, ye behold that the Lord is with us; and ye behold that he has
delivered you into our hands. And now I would that ye should understand that this is done unto us *because of our religion and our faith
in Christ*. And now ye see that ye cannot destroy this our faith. Now
ye see that this is the true faith of God; yea, ye see that God will
support, and keep, and preserve us, so long as we are faithful unto
him, and unto our faith, and our religion; and never will the Lord
suffer that we shall be destroyed except we should fall into transgression and deny our faith." (Alma 44:3–4, italics added.)

The relative importance of righteousness versus armaments
was clearly explained by President Spencer W. Kimball:

O foolish men who think to protect the world with armaments, battleships, and space equipment, when only righteousness is needed!

The answer to all of our problems—personal, national, and
international—has been given to us many times by many
prophets, ancient and modern. . . . Perhaps it is too simple for
us to see. We look to foreign programs, summit conferences,
land bases. We depend on fortifications, or gods of stone; upon
ships and planes and projectiles, our gods of iron—gods which

have no ears, no eyes, no hearts. We pray to them for deliverance and depend upon them for protection . . . like the gods of Baal.

God will fight our battles if we honor him and serve him with all our hearts, might, mind, and strength.

President Kimball also taught that "a one-sided disarmament could be madness if worldliness and materialism continued, but a serious turn of the masses could forestall all military conquests, all tragedies of conflict. God is all-powerful." He warned us about our personal attitudes when he declared: "We are a warlike people, easily distracted from our assignment of preparing for the coming of the Lord. . . . When threatened, we become antienemy instead of pro-kingdom of God." (*The Teachings of Spencer W. Kimball*, ed. Edward L. Kimball [Salt Lake City: Bookcraft, 1982], pp. 416–17.)

Involvement in war does not need to bring hate, bitterness, and insensitivity. War can actually bring us closer to God if our motives and desires are right. This was clearly taught by Mormon: "Many had become hardened, because of the exceedingly great length of the war; and many were softened because of their afflictions, insomuch that they did humble themselves before God, even in the depth of humility" (Alma 62:41).

In war, as in every other struggle and conflict in our lives, the basic principles of the gospel apply. Hate is always self-destructive, and love is always spiritually and emotionally renewing. If we need to go to war, through prayer we can draw close to God and counter the hatred and cruelty that some develop, so long as our desires and motives are true. By doing this, not only do we adjust more quickly and successfully when the war is over but we find ourselves able to teach and assist those who were considered our enemies. With the help of God we can always remain "pro-kingdom of God" instead of "antienemy."

Chapter 49

TRUE AT
ALL TIMES

ALMA 53:20–21

W hile Marianne was vacationing in New Zealand she backed her car into a parked car in the hotel parking lot. Because the damage was slight—about one inch of paint was scraped off the other car—and because she was down to her last four dollars, she quickly left the parking lot without leaving any kind of note or identification.

When she arrived in her room she knelt in prayer to ask God if not doing anything was okay. As soon as she closed her eyes she knew she was in the wrong, and she asked God for his help in doing the right thing. She wrote a note leaving her name and room number and placed it on the car.

Marianne enjoyed a good night's sleep because she was right with herself and with God. The owner of the car contacted her the next morning, told her that the damage to his car was insignificant, and explained how pleased he was that she had left a note.

When her family learned about the incident she was grateful that she had done the correct thing. As she explained how she had gone to her room intending to avoid responsibility for what she had done, her daughter said, "Mother, I know you, and you would never do that!"

Marianne once again felt the joy that comes to us when we are true to ourselves and, therefore, true to our families, to others, and to the Lord. (See Marianne Flint, *Ensign*, January 1990, p. 64.)

This same trait of personal integrity was demonstrated by the stripling warriors: "And they were all young men, and they were exceedingly valiant for courage, and also for strength and activity; but behold, this was not all—they were men who were *true at all times in whatsoever thing they were entrusted.* Yea, they were men of truth and soberness, for they had been taught to keep the commandments of God and to walk uprightly before him." (Alma 53:20–21, italics added.)

The words "walk uprightly before him" are significant and important to every one of us. When we are true to ourselves we can face God, ourselves, and others with a clear conscience. President Howard W. Hunter stressed the importance of being true to ourselves: "The ability to stand by one's principles, to live with integrity and faith according to one's belief—that is what matters, that is the difference between a contribution and a commitment. That devotion to true principle—in our individual lives, in our homes and families, and in all places that we meet and influence other people—that devotion is what God is ultimately requesting of us." (*Ensign,* May 1990, p. 61.)

Marianne did not allow the size of the scrape or her financial situation to determine whether she would be true to herself. Integrity and honesty are not determined by size but by commitment. Integrity—or the lack of it—can be demonstrated by something as small as a dime or a doughnut. When we are devoted and committed to the gospel of Jesus Christ we are "true at all times in whatsoever thing [we are] entrusted." If we falter in one area, chances are we are weak in other areas as well. Integrity is demonstrated by consistency.

Bishop J. Richard Clarke mentioned one man who recognized the need for such moral consistency:

> General David Shoup, former Commandant of the United States Marine Corps, felt very strongly about consistency in practicing moral values. Commenting upon marines who were untrue to their wives, he said:
>
> "It is not the actual act of adultery that is of so great a concern to me; that's merely the by-product, so to speak. The vital thing is this: A man who can somehow rationalize breaking the oath he gave before God and man when he repeated the marriage vows, is also a man who could, if he so desired, or when subjected to sufficient pressure, rationalize breaking the oath

he took when he became a Commissioned Officer in the United States Marine Corps. A man who can betray his wife and children for lustful purposes is a man who could betray his country for his own ends." (*Ensign*, May 1984, p. 63.)

None of us is perfect, and all of us perform below our ideals, but if we find ourselves rationalizing our involvement in some forms of sin, it may be an indication that we need to shore up our integrity and commitment to the gospel of Christ. Some who would refuse to watch R-rated movies would sit through PG-rated movies filled with vulgarity and sexual innuendos. Others who would never swear at home swear often in the workplace. Sometimes those who seem to be totally committed to honesty in their personal lives will cheat on their income taxes or use questionable business practices. We may feel that our word is our bond to others but break promises we make to our spouse or children. As we think about the integrity demonstrated by Marianne and the stripling warriors, we may want to evaluate our own commitment and consider our own consistency when it comes to being faithful to the values we know to be true.

Chapter 50

YE MAY
REMEMBER THEM

HELAMAN 5:4–7

The following verses explain why Helaman named his sons Nephi and Lehi and the effect for good it had on their lives:

> And it came to pass that Nephi had become weary because of their iniquity; and he yielded up the judgment-seat, and took it upon him to preach the word of God all the remainder of his days, and his brother Lehi also, all the remainder of his days;
>
> For they remembered the words which their father Helaman spake unto them. And these are the words which he spake:
>
> Behold, my sons, I desire that ye should remember to keep the commandments of God; and I would that ye should declare unto the people these words. Behold, I have given unto you the names of our first parents who came out of the land of Jerusalem; and this I have done that when you remember your names ye may remember them; and when ye remember them ye may remember their works; and when ye remember their works ye may know how that it is said, and also written, that they were good.
>
> Therefore, my sons, I would that ye should do that which is good, that it may be said of you, and also written, even as it has been said and written of them. (Helaman 5:4–7.)

Helaman realized the great importance of a good name. A person's name should be among his most treasured possessions. It represents who he is and what he stands for. When someone hears your name mentioned, an image or an impression of the person he thinks you are is instantly brought to his mind. This image can be a positive or a negative one, and it is usually based on the things you have said and done.

What a person does with his name affects every member of his family. President N. Eldon Tanner had an experience that caused him to decide that he was going to keep his name clean so that his posterity might benefit from an "unsullied name." He needed to borrow some money so that he could go to school and become a teacher. He was "frightened to death" as he went to the bank and asked the manager for the loan. The banker asked him who he was, and he said that he was Eldon Tanner. When the banker asked him if he was "So-and-So's boy," he replied that he was not but was the son of N. W. Tanner.

The manager asked him when he could repay the money, and he indicated that as soon as he started teaching he would pay it back as quickly as possible. The bank manager then said, "If you are N. W. Tanner's son, I'm prepared to let you have the money." No security other than his father's name was needed. (See Leon R. Hartshorn, comp., *Outstanding Stories by General Authorities*, vol. 1 [Salt Lake City: Deseret Book Co., 1970], pp. 203–4.)

As members of the kingdom of God we also carry the name of Christ. When we took upon ourselves the name of Christ we promised that we would give ourselves wholeheartedly to his service. When we perform acts of charity, love, and kindness, positive feelings are generated towards his church, and people are brought closer to God. When we give in to daily temptation and stimuli, the progress of the Church is curtailed and people are driven further from the truth.

Several years ago a new high school principal in a small community decided to find out which students were respected most by their peers. He had the four hundred students in the school each fill out a brief questionnaire in which they listed the three or four students they admired and respected the most. He also asked them to explain what these students had done to earn this respect.

This school, like all schools, was made up of many different types and groups of students. There were athletes, smokers and "druggies," handicapped students, popular and unpopular students, slow learners and high achievers, middle-of-the-road Joes and Janes, Latter-day Saints and non-Latter-day Saints, religious and nonreligious students, and many others. The amazing result of this survey was that one Latter-day Saint girl was listed first on most of the papers and was at least named by every student in the school. Because of her sincere concern for and friendliness toward every student in the school, she was in a position to influence their lives. She accepted everyone as they were and, therefore, could help them become better people. Her name, years later, is still remembered for good by the teachers and students that she associated with. And because she was an active member of the Lord's church, the Church benefited as well.

If we live the gospel the way we should, our names will be associated with honesty, virtue, kindness, and with the many other attributes of concerned Latter-day Saints. This will be a great blessing not just to ourselves but to our family and to the Lord as well. There are very few things so valuable as a good name.

Chapter 51

YE ARE
ANGRY WITH HIM

HELAMAN 13:26–28

Even though most of us do not like being told we are doing things that are wrong and that we need to change, it can be a great blessing to us. It gives us a chance to alter our course and to get back on the path that leads to eternal life. Prophets are among the best friends we ever have because they help us make adjustments that bring increased blessings and happiness. Yet, throughout history many have rejected the living prophets because their messages have demanded repentance and effort. The prophet Samuel described this attitude:

> If a prophet come among you and declareth unto you the word of the Lord, which testifieth of your sins and iniquities, ye are angry with him, and cast him out and seek all manner of ways to destroy him; yea, you will say that he is a false prophet, and that he is a sinner, and of the devil, because he testifieth that your deeds are evil.
>
> But behold, if a man shall come among you and shall say: Do this, and there is no iniquity; do that and ye shall not suffer; yea, he will say: Walk after the pride of your own hearts; yea, walk after the pride of your eyes, and do whatsoever your heart desireth—and if a man shall come among you and say this, ye will receive him, and say that he is a prophet.
>
> . . . Because he speaketh flattering words unto you, and he

saith that all is well, then ye will not find fault with him. (Helaman 13:26–28.)

Some people seem to have "figured out" how to tell when a prophet is speaking as a prophet and when he is just speaking as a man. If they agree with what he is saying, he must be speaking as a prophet; but if they disagree, he is just speaking as a man. As they reject the words of the prophet they also reject the Lord and the blessings promised the faithful.

Another problem described by Samuel was "faith" in dead prophets but the rejection of living ones. A few years ago a Gospel Doctrine teacher read statements by both Joseph Smith and the living prophet concerning salvation of children. A member of the class, who was also one of the ward priesthood leaders, declared that he did not believe the doctrine taught by these men and would not believe it unless the same doctrine was taught by one of the prophets in the Bible. This man accepted the teachings of dead prophets but rejected those of the current one.

Elder James E. Faust said: "I do not believe members of this church can be in full harmony with the Savior without sustaining his living prophet on the earth, the President of the Church. If we do not sustain the living prophet, whoever he may be, we die spiritually. Ironically, some have died spiritually by exclusively following prophets who have long been dead. Others equivocate in their support of living prophets, trying to lift themselves up by putting down the living prophets, however subtly."

Elder Faust also quoted President George Q. Cannon as saying: "We have the Bible, the Book of Mormon and the Book of Doctrine and Covenants; but all these books, without the living oracles and a constant stream of revelation from the Lord, would not lead any people into the Celestial Kingdom." (*Ensign,* November 1989, pp. 9–10.)

It is not just by raising our hands at conference but by accepting and applying the counsel of the living prophet that we sustain him. When the living prophet talked about the role of women in the home, some members of the Church said he was old-fashioned and didn't understand today's financial needs. When the priesthood was made available to every worthy male, dissenters claimed that social pressure, not revelation, had led to the change. When the prophet spoke against increased military buildup and stressed the importance of spiritual preparation, many rejected his words because they were political in nature.

It is important for all of us to clarify our role and the role of the prophet. The role of the prophet is to receive revelation and inspiration from the Lord, and our role is to find out that he is a prophet and then follow him. We are wise when we follow the instructions of the Lord, as revealed through the prophet, regardless of whether we are in total agreement at the time. When we disagree with a prophet it may indicate one of two problems: either we do not really believe he is a prophet, or we feel that we have more insight and knowledge on the issue than God. Either of these possibilities is unacceptable to a faithful follower of Christ.

God wants us to follow his prophets, but he does not want us to follow them blindly. He wants each of us to gain a personal spiritual witness of the living prophet and of his teachings and counsel. Once we know that the prophet is truly the Lord's representative and that his counsel comes from the Lord, we can move ahead with greater confidence in doing what he asks us to do. As we follow the counsel of the prophet we are literally doing the will of the Lord. What a blessing it is to have living prophets who help us apply the gospel principles in the circumstances we face today!

Chapter 52

ONE BY ONE

3 NEPHI 11, 17

Margaret was very sick with the flu and had no one to help her. Her family had recently moved into town; she had no family members or friends who were close, and her husband was out of town on business. Just the effort of fixing a quick breakfast for her two sons caused her to shake with chills and fever as she collapsed on her bed.

Within a few hours her difficulties escalated as her one-year-old developed a high fever and demanded her constant attention. Margaret was so sick herself that this added burden caused her to feel extremely frustrated and depressed. When the doorbell rang she felt a glimmer of hope that it might be someone who would see her situation and offer to help.

The person at the door was a neighbor, a ward member named Sister Cook. With her sick child clutched to her chest and her two-year-old hanging from her robe, Margaret cried out in relief, "Oh, Sister Cook, I'm so glad to see you! I'm not feeling well, and now I think I've given it to Kelly too."

Sister Cook's response was not exactly what Margaret had hoped for. She said, "Oh, that's too bad, dear. I am sorry to hear that. I just came by to ask you to help in my Relief Society lesson next week. I'm the social relations teacher, you know." Sister Cook then handed Margaret a paper with some writing on it and said, "Thank you so much, and now I really must be going. Sister McAllister and I are doing our visiting teaching this morning. I hope you get to feeling better. Good-bye now."

After closing the door Margaret "walked numbly into the living room and sank on the couch with Kelly. Trying to remain composed, Margaret glanced at the paper she had crumpled in her shaky hand. The heading in bold type read: 'FEED MY SHEEP.' " (See Darla Larsen Hanks, *Ensign*, April 1979, p. 15.)

Sometimes we get so caught up in meetings and structured programs that we look beyond the mark. The whole purpose of meetings and programs is to help and bless the *one*. I learned years ago as a seminary teacher that I don't teach classes but thirty individual "ones" sitting in the classroom. Sister Cook was so caught up in teaching about feeding the sheep that she failed to recognize and nurture a lamb that was in need. Her visiting teaching would look good on the report, but a daughter of God went unassisted.

Jesus wanted us to realize the importance of each individual child of God. Nowhere is his love and concern for each of us better revealed than in his visit to the Nephites on the American continent. When we realize that there were approximately twenty-five hundred Nephites that he ministered to, his concern for the one becomes even more powerful and enlightening. After Jesus had introduced himself and the people had fallen to the earth, he said to them:

> Arise and come forth unto me, that ye may thrust your hands into my side, and also that ye may feel the prints of the nails in my hands and in my feet, that ye may know that I am the God of Israel, and the God of the whole earth, and have been slain for the sins of the world.
>
> And it came to pass that the multitude went forth, and thrust their hands into his side, and did feel the prints of the nails in his hands and in his feet; and this they did do, going forth *one by one* until they had all gone forth, and did see with their eyes and did feel with their hands, and did know of a surety and did bear record, that it was he, of whom it was written by the prophets, that should come. (3 Nephi 11:14–15, italics added.)

For twenty-five hundred people to quietly and reverently approach the Savior and personally make both physical and spiritual contact with him must have taken some time, yet the Savior wanted each of them to experience this special blessing.

After calling the twelve Nephite disciples and teaching the people many things, Jesus said he would leave them and return again on the morrow. But as he looked around at the people he could tell that they did not want him to leave, and he was filled with compassion. He then said:

> Have ye any that are sick among you? Bring them hither. Have ye any that are lame, or blind, or halt, or maimed, or leprous, or that are withered, or that are deaf, or that are afflicted in any manner? Bring them hither and I will heal them, for I have compassion upon you; my bowels are filled with mercy.
>
> For I perceive that ye desire that I should show unto you what I have done unto your brethren at Jerusalem, for I see that your faith is sufficient that I should heal you.
>
> And it came to pass that when he had thus spoken, all the multitude, with one accord, did go forth with their sick and their afflicted, and their lame, and with their blind, and with their dumb, and with all them that were afflicted in any manner; and he did heal them *every one as they were brought forth unto him.* (3 Nephi 17:7–9, italics added.)

Later that same day Jesus "took their little children, one by one, and blessed them, and prayed unto the Father for them. And when he had done this he wept again," because of his joy. (See 3 Nephi 17:20–22.)

Jesus could have healed the people and blessed the children as a group, but by taking the time to bless each one individually he revealed his own concern for each individual person and taught us the importance of reaching out to the one.

Ned Winder, who served as executive secretary of the Missionary Department, told President Thomas S. Monson the following experience. Brother Winder was walking down a staircase with two of the General Authorities when they were spotted by a mother and her young son. The boy asked his mother who the first man was, and she told him that he was Elder Marvin J. Ashton, a member of the Council of the Twelve Apostles. In answer to his question concerning who the second man was, he was informed that he was Elder Loren C. Dunn, of the First Quorum of the Seventy. When the boy asked who the third man was, the mother lowered her voice and said, "Oh, he's nobody." (See Thomas S. Monson, *Ensign*, May 1989, p. 43.)

Brother Winder did not take offense but felt this was quite humorous; however, the mother could not have been more wrong. In the heart of God there is no such person as "nobody." Every one of us is precious and valuable in the sight of God. And every person should be of great worth to each one of us. As we concentrate less on the group and more on each member that makes up the group, our service, both in and out of the Church, will become much more rewarding and many times more effective.

Chapter 53

AND THEY
WERE FILLED

3 NEPHI 18:3-11

R obert, who was a soldier in Vietnam, had been on patrol for three or four weeks and was waiting to be airlifted out for a rest. Many of his friends had been killed or wounded as his company had chased the Vietcong by day and been attacked by them at night. As he lay in a ditch, trying to avoid a sniper's rifle fire, he heard someone whistling a familiar melody, which he finally recognized as "We Thank Thee, O God, for a Prophet."

Robert quickly looked around and found that the whistling was coming from a private who had just arrived by helicopter. He crawled over to him and soon discovered that he was a Latter-day Saint and that he held the priesthood. This was the first member of the Church Robert had been in touch with in months. Robert knew by his calendar watch that it was the Sabbath, and he asked this fellow member if he would participate in a sacrament service with him.

The two men crawled out of the ditch into some tall grass where they could have total privacy, and they prepared for the sacrament. A helmet was used for the table and a white handkerchief for the sacrament cloth. A C-ration biscuit and water from a canteen became the sacrament emblems, and the prayers were read out of a serviceman's copy of *Principles of the Gospel*.

As the two soldiers knelt together in the mud Robert broke and blessed the bread while the other soldier watched the jungle with his rifle ready. After the bread was eaten the water was blessed while Robert stood guard. Robert explained the effect this sacred ordinance had upon his soul:

> Never in my life has the bread of the sacrament tasted so sweet and the water so pure as it did that day, nor has my soul been so strengthened by the ordinance. We clasped hands, then quickly crawled back to the protection of the ditch. Immediately the whine of the helicopters again filled the air, and I was up and running for the landing zone with the other members of my squad. I turned and looked back, my fear gone, and he smiled and gave the "thumbs-up" signal. I climbed aboard the HUEY, and we were gone.
>
> I never asked that soldier's name, nor he mine, but in those brief moments we forged a bond to last throughout eternity. That fellow Saint had rescued my soul from the horror and despair of war. Partaking of the sacrament in the jungle had brought me closer to the Lord than I had ever been before.
>
> Through a gospel ordinance, we had found peace. (Robert K. Hillman, *Ensign*, April 1989, pp. 10–11.)

When we prepare ourselves and partake of the sacrament with the same intensity and desire as Robert, we receive the same blessings of peace, spiritual strength, and closeness to God.

The blessings that come from worthily and sincerely partaking of the sacrament are referred to in the verses that relate Christ's introduction of the sacrament to the Nephite people: "And when the disciples had come with bread and wine, he took of the bread and brake and blessed it; and he gave unto the disciples and commanded that they should eat. And when they had eaten and were *filled*, he commanded that they should give unto the multitude." After the multitude ate and "were filled," Jesus told the people one would be ordained to administer the sacrament and that all members of his Church should partake of the sacrament.

Jesus then taught the Nephites: "This shall ye do in remembrance of my body, which I have shown unto you. And it shall be a testimony unto the Father that ye do always remember me. And if ye do always remember me ye shall *have my Spirit to be with you*." (3 Nephi 18:3–7, italics added.)

This description of how the Nephites partook of the bread and "were filled" implies that they were filled with the Holy Ghost and received the same blessings that Robert and his companion received. The Holy Ghost conveys peace and strength to our souls and brings us closer to our Heavenly Father.

Because many of us will take the sacrament more than thirty-five hundred times before we leave this life, we may tend to take this ordinance for granted, but just the opposite should be true. If we are going to covenant more than thirty-five hundred times that we will take upon us the name of Christ, always remember him, and keep his commandments, we had better take this covenant seriously.

The importance of striving to keep this covenant and, therefore, of partaking of the sacrament worthily was discussed by President David O. McKay, who warned: "To partake of the sacrament unworthily is to take a step toward spiritual death. No man can be dishonest within himself without deadening the susceptibility of his spirit. . . . He who promises one thing and deliberately fails to keep his word adds sin to sin. On natural principles such a man 'eats and drinks condemnation to his soul,' for true life consists in obedience to the principles of the gospel, and we promise when we partake of the sacrament to keep those principles." (*Improvement Era*, January 1953, p. 14.)

We are usually worthy to partake of the sacrament if the desires and intentions of our hearts are right. As we use the sacrament time to contemplate and to pray silently about our lives and our relationship with God and others, we may become aware of areas of our lives that need improving. We should commit ourselves to work hard to overcome these weaknesses and ask God to help and strengthen us. We can then partake of the sacrament worthily, knowing that we desire to do God's will and keep his commandments. Partaking of the sacrament worthily has more to do with repentance, effort, and improvement than it does with flawlessness and perfection.

Occasionally priesthood leaders are directed by the Spirit to restrict sacrament participation because of sins of a more serious nature. Elder John H. Groberg described how one sister, who had received this restriction, felt when she was able to again participate in this sacred ordinance, and he also explained the attitude that made her worthy to again partake of the sacrament.

Sister Jones sat again with her family, nervous, yet excited and full of anticipation. "Am I really worthy? How I want to be!" she thought. The sacrament hymn was more meaningful than ever. She sang with such feeling that it was difficult to hold back the tears. And the sacrament prayers—how profound! She listened so intently that every word sank deep into her soul—to take his name, always remember him, keep his commandments, always have his Spirit. (See D&C 20:77, 79.) "Oh, how I desire this," she thought.

The deacons began to move up and down the aisles, and the trays were passed from person to person across the rows. As one young deacon got closer and closer to her row, her heart began to pound harder and harder. Then the tray was coming down her very row. Now her husband was holding the tray in front of her! Tears streamed down her face. There was a barely audible sob of joy. "Oh!" as she reached for the emblem of the Lord's love for her. The congregation did not hear the sob, but they did notice the tears in the bishop's eyes. (*Ensign*, May 1989, p. 39.)

Sister Jones received great spiritual strength from her partaking of the sacrament because she had prepared herself and because she was worthy. She truly wanted to have the Spirit of the Lord and to keep his commandments. Because her heart was right she received a forgiveness of her sins and the companionship of the Holy Ghost. As we approach the sacrament with the same intensity and desire to keep our baptismal commitments and to serve the Lord, these same blessings will be ours.

Chapter 54

WATCH
AND PRAY

3 NEPHI 18:18

It is claimed that you cannot kill a frog by dropping him into boiling water, because as soon as he feels the heat he jumps out and escapes. However, if the frog is placed in cold water and the temperature of the water is then gradually increased until the water is scalding, the frog will not realize what is happening to him, and he will be cooked before he even knows he is in danger.

Satan understands this principle well and uses it often on each of us. He knows that we will not lower our standards all at once, so he tempts us to lower them just a little at a time. Jesus warned the Nephite people of Satan's strategy when he said: "Ye must watch and pray always lest ye enter into temptation; for Satan desireth to have you, that he may sift you as wheat" (3 Nephi 18:18).

If Satan can get us just to "enter into" some kind of mild sin, he can then slowly—but surely—entice us to increase our involvement until we are immersed much more deeply in sin than we ever felt possible. This is why we need to not only pray but watch and be on guard as well. President Spencer W. Kimball warned that "the adversary is so smart and subtle that he takes every man in his own game. The man whose weakness is money will be led inch by inch and yard by yard and mile by mile into that area where his wants can be satisfied. If one's ambition is power, the evil one knows exactly how to build him up to that point. If one's weakness is sex, Satan in his erudition and experience and brilliance knows a thousand reasons why sex may be liberated to run rampant and express itself and satisfy itself. Lucifer is real. He is subtle. He is convincing. He is powerful." (*The Teachings of Spencer W. Kimball,* ed. Edward L. Kimball [Salt Lake City: Bookcraft, 1982], p. 151.)

The importance of watching and praying constantly and of being on guard against even the smallest improprieties was sadly demonstrated by two Church leaders who were quietly and deviously led where they never consciously wanted to go. They held important positions—one in the Young Women organization and the other in the Young Men organization—and they occasionally found themselves away from their families at youth activities. Once when a dance was held for the youth they saw nothing wrong with dancing a few times with each other and visiting quietly in the corner during the remainder of the dance.

After returning home they found reasons why they needed to meet with one another in order to fulfill their Church responsibilities. These meetings took place without other members of the presidencies, who should have been invited. Their discussions became increasingly personal in nature. One day they decided to meet for a harmless lunch in a neighboring city. This lunch was followed by other lunches and other indiscretions until they lost their chastity and their membership in the Church. Innocent family members were injured, and wounds were opened that took many years and much effort to heal. Like the frog in the boiling water, these two good people ended up where they never wanted to be because they allowed Satan to turn up the heat just a little at a time. They could have avoided the whole situation by never "getting in the pot."

As powerful as Satan is, God's power is greater. Satan's subtle and cunning ruses can be exposed by the personal revelation and inspiration promised to come to each of us as we watch and pray and strive to keep the commandments. With the help of the Holy Ghost we can come to recognize Satan's hot or cold water for what it is and keep both large and small sins out of our lives.

Chapter 55

POUR YOU
OUT A BLESSING

3 NEPHI 24:8–11

When Elder Bernard P. Brockbank and his wife had a young family, they did not pay their tithing because they were struggling financially. One day his wife asked him, "Do you love God?" When he answered that he did she asked, "Do you love God as much as you love the grocer?"

Elder Brockbank indicated that he hoped he loved him more than the grocer, and she replied, "But you paid the grocer. Do you love God as much as the landlord? You paid him, didn't you?" She then pointed out that the first and great commandment was to love God and that they had not paid their tithing. They repented, paid their tithing, and received great blessings from the Lord. (See *Ensign*, June 1971, p. 86.)

A great truth about tithing is that it has much more to do with love, faith, and obedience than it does with money. Everything on this earth belongs to God, and when we fail to pay our tithes and offerings we demonstrate not only a deficiency in faith and love but a lack of appreciation as well. Maybe that is why God used such strong language when he said: "Will a man rob God? Yet ye have robbed me. But ye say: Wherein have we robbed thee? In tithes and offerings. Ye are cursed with a curse, for ye have robbed me, even this whole nation." (3 Nephi 24:8–9.)

It is not so much that God needs our money as that the non-payment of tithes reveals serious flaws in our character and spiritual maturity. In section 59 of the Doctrine and Covenants, God indicated that nothing offends him more than those who are not grateful for the blessings that he bestows upon them (see D&C 59:21).

Because of the promised blessings of tithing, obedience to this principle really is a matter of faith. The Lord said: "Bring ye all the tithes into the storehouse, that there may be meat in my house; and prove me now herewith, saith the Lord of Hosts, if I will not open you the windows of heaven, and *pour you out a blessing* that there shall not be room enough to receive it. And I will rebuke the devourer for your sakes, and he shall not destroy the fruits of your ground; neither shall your vine cast her fruit before the time in the fields, saith the Lord of Hosts." (3 Nephi 24:10–11, italics added.)

Both spiritual and physical blessings are promised to those who willingly and generously obey the law of tithes and offerings. A person who says he cannot afford to pay tithing is saying, in a very real way, that he does not believe the Lord will bless and help him. Because of his lack of faith, he is unwilling to prove the Lord. Those who have obeyed this commandment, even when they didn't see how they would be able to take care of the needs of their families, have received the help that the Lord has promised. They no longer have faith just in the law of tithing; they have found for themselves that the Lord's promises will *all* be fulfilled.

One Church leader asked the members of a congregation how many of them would die for the Church. Most of the members raised their hands. He then asked how many of them paid a full tithing, and only about a third of the hands went up. He then said, "Apparently, most of you would rather die than pay tithing." This story is somewhat humorous, but it points out the importance of living for the Church rather than dying for it.

One young man who was willing to live for the Church was a sixteen-year-old priest named Roger Smith. When a local radio station informed him that he had won a brand new Corvette Stingray, the first thing he said after hanging up the phone was, "Now my mission is paid for, but how do you tithe a car?" He later took cash, paid tithing on it, and placed the rest in a bank account for his mission. (See Victor L. Brown, *New Era*, July 1975, p. 5.)

The faith and love that this young man demonstrated is shown by thousands of members—from the very young to the very old— who faithfully and willingly pay a full and honest tithing on a regular basis. Nearly all of these people could share several accounts of having been blessed financially by the Lord, and all of them can bear testimony of spiritual blessings that they have received. Those who have proven the Lord have received much more than they ever gave.

Chapter 56

BUILT UPON
MY GOSPEL

3 NEPHI 27:13–22

Many years ago a Church member married and went east to live. When each of her neighbors learned she was a member of the Mormon church, they wanted to know what Mormons believed.

Not knowing where to turn for help, this young woman wrote to the editor of the question-and-answer page in the *Deseret News*. She pleaded with the editor to tell her about the teachings of the Church. She said that she knew the first two principles of the gospel: you should not use tea and coffee, and you should not play cards.

This story has not been included to ridicule this person, who sincerely wanted to better understand the teachings of the Church, but to emphasize a problem many of us may have. This is the problem of getting bogged down in peripheral teachings and never fully comprehending the core of the gospel. Jesus taught the Nephites the heart and essence of the gospel in the following verses:

> Behold I have given unto you my gospel, and *this is the gospel* which I have given unto you—that I came into the world to do the will of my Father, because my Father sent me.
>
> And my Father sent me that I might be lifted up upon the cross; and after that I had been lifted up upon the cross, that might draw all men unto me . . . to stand before me, to be judged of their works, whether they be good or whether they be evil. . . .

And it shall come to pass, that whoso repenteth and is baptized in my name shall be filled; and if he endureth to the end, behold, him will I hold guiltless before my Father at that day when I shall stand to judge the world. (3 Nephi 27:13–14, 16, italics added.)

The gospel is the good news that because Christ suffered for our sins and was resurrected, we can repent, be resurrected, and receive eternal life. The gospel principles that assist us in partaking of these great blessings are faith in the Lord Jesus Christ, repentance, baptism by immersion by one having authority, and receiving and responding to the Holy Ghost. Through the atonement of Christ and the reception of the Holy Ghost we can become clean and spotless before God.

A fifth step often mentioned by Christ is the process of enduring to the end, which is the process of remaining clean and spotless. We do this by abiding in our faith, continuing in the repentance process, keeping our baptismal covenants, and responding continually to the promptings of the Spirit.

Sometimes people build their spiritual and religious lives on unsteady foundations. Some may join the Church because of an outstanding missionary or a good Latter-day Saint neighbor. Others may be converted because of programs such as Relief Society, the sports program, or Scouting. The emphasis on families may be the thing that causes some to join the Church. There may be many different things that first attract people to the Lord's church, but no one is on safe ground until he receives a spiritual conversion and builds his testimony on basic gospel principles that center around Christ and his atonement.

Helaman referred to the importance of this kind of foundation: "And now, my sons, remember, remember that it is upon the rock of our Redeemer, who is Christ, the Son of God, that ye must build your foundation; that when the devil shall send forth his mighty winds, yea, his shafts in the whirlwind, yea, when all his hail and his mighty storm shall beat upon you, it shall have no power over you to drag you down to the gulf of misery and endless wo, because of the rock upon which ye are built, which is a sure foundation, *a foundation whereon if men build they cannot fall*" (Helaman 5:12, italics added).

Chapter 57

SORROWING
OF THE DAMNED

MORMON 2:12–13

A fifteen-year-old girl had lost her chastity and was feeling the anguish of a guilty conscience. She had read one of my books for teenagers and wrote me asking what she could do to get rid of her torment. I explained to her how she could become clean and encouraged her to go to her bishop, but she was hesitant to follow my counsel. We exchanged several letters, and I tried to help her see the path that she needed to follow in order to have her virtue restored and her pain relieved. When her letters quit coming I tried to locate her, even though she lived in another city, but I was unable to do so. As I reread her letters I realized that she wanted to get rid of the pain but continue in the path that she had chosen. She felt sorrow, but it was not the sorrow that leads to complete repentance.

Mormon referred to such unrepentant sorrow as the "sorrowing of the damned." The Nephites had become extremely wicked, until they had lost all of the help and protection that God promises the righteous. The face of the land was covered with blood and carnage, and the robbers and murderers had become so prevalent that "no man could keep that which was his own." Mormon described their condition in the following words:

> And it came to pass that when I, Mormon, saw their lamentation and their mourning and their sorrow before the Lord,

my heart did begin to rejoice within me, knowing the mercies and the long-suffering of the Lord, therefore supposing that he would be merciful unto them that they would again become a righteous people.

But behold this my joy was vain, for their sorrowing was not unto repentance, because of the goodness of God; but it was rather the sorrowing of the damned, because the Lord would not always suffer them to take happiness in sin. (Mormon 2:12–13.)

The scriptures talk about another type of sorrow, called godly sorrow, which leads us to repentance and to total forgiveness. President Ezra Taft Benson identified and explained both types of sorrow:

It is not uncommon to find men and women in the world who feel remorse for the things they do wrong. Sometimes this is because their actions cause them or loved ones great sorrow and misery. Sometimes their sorrow is caused because they are caught and punished for their actions. Such worldly feelings do not constitute "godly sorrow." . . .

Godly sorrow is a gift of the Spirit. It is a deep realization that our actions have offended our Father and our God. It is the sharp and keen awareness that our behavior caused the Savior, He who knew no sin, even the greatest of all, to endure agony and suffering. Our sins caused Him to bleed at every pore. This very real mental and spiritual anguish is what the scriptures refer to as having "a broken heart and a contrite spirit." Such a spirit is the absolute prerequisite for true repentance. (*Ensign,* October 1989, p. 4.)

Sometimes people turn from their negative behavior, for any number of reasons, and then feel that they are repentant and forgiven. Elder Vaughn J. Featherstone told about one young man who seemed to be proud and even boastful of his past transgressions. This young man wanted to go on a mission but, because of his serious transgressions, needed to be cleared by a General Authority. When the young man was asked why he felt he should be cleared for a mission, he responded that he had not committed his past sins for a year, so he was forgiven and worthy to go.

He was very surprised when Elder Featherstone said, "I'm sorry to tell you this but you are *not* going on a mission. Do you suppose we could send you out with your braggadocio attitude about this past life of yours, boasting of your escapades? . . . What you have committed is a series of monumental transgressions. You haven't repented; you've just stopped doing something. Someday, after you have been to Gethsemane and back, you'll understand what true repentance is."

Six months later, following a fireside presentation, Elder Featherstone was approached by this young man. As they shook hands, he could see that an important change had taken place in the young man's life. Tears were streaming down his cheeks, and an "almost holy glow came from his countenance."

When Elder Featherstone said, "You've been there, haven't you!" the response was, "Yes, I've been to Gethsemane and back." The boy then thanked Elder Featherstone for helping him to do the things that led him to complete forgiveness. (See Vaughn J. Featherstone, *A Generation of Excellence: A Guide for Parents and Youth Leaders* [Salt Lake City: Bookcraft, 1975], pp. 156–159.)

Since godly sorrow leads us to actions that will bring full and complete repentance, it is a great blessing to us. Godly sorrow comes through the ministering of the Holy Ghost as we realize and comprehend the great gift of the Atonement and the love that God and Christ have for us personally. One active Church member spent fifty long years suffering for her sins as a teenager but never felt godly sorrow until she read *The Miracle of Forgiveness*, by President Spencer W. Kimball, and realized how much she owed the Savior. She then approached her bishop and cleared the burden of guilt she had carried for so many years. A few days later she called her bishop and thanked him for helping her feel straight with the Lord and good about herself.

Since godly sorrow comes from the Spirit, we can pray that we will be sensitive to the pain that accompanies sin. Just as physical pain alerts us to physical harm the Holy Ghost warns us, through our conscience, when we are damaging ourselves spiritually. We can then make the proper adjustments in our lives and divert the serious spiritual damage that takes place when we ignore feelings of guilt and the whisperings of the Spirit.

Chapter 58

TO GET
POWER AND GAIN

ETHER 8:15–23

One of the most devastating problems the Book of Mormon people faced was secret combinations. These combinations brought immense suffering and sin and eventually led to the total destruction of both the Jaredite and the Nephite nations. Moroni tells us that they were handed down from the time of Cain and "kept up by the power of the devil" in order to help "such as sought power to gain power, and to murder, and to plunder, and to lie, and to commit all manner of wickedness and whoredoms." (See Ether 8:15–16.)

Moroni then warned us that "whatsoever nation shall uphold such secret combinations, to get power and gain, until they shall spread over the nation, behold, they shall be destroyed." (Ether 8:22.)

A better understanding of these combinations and of how to avoid them can be gained by studying the first combination, which was established between Satan and Cain. The scriptures indicate that Cain, his wife, and many of his brethren, loved Satan more than God. Because Cain hated his brother Abel, and because he desired his brother's flocks, he made a pact with Satan: "Satan said unto Cain: Swear unto me by thy throat, and if thou tell it thou shalt die; and swear thy brethren by their heads, and by the living God, that they tell it not; for if they tell it, they shall surely die; and this that thy father may not know it; and this day I will deliver thy brother Abel into thine hands. . . . And all these things were done in secret. And Cain said: Truly I am Mahan, the master of this great secret, that I may murder and get gain. Wherefore Cain was called Master Mahan, and he gloried in his wickedness." (Moses 5:29–31.)

At the very heart of these combinations was—and is—the desire to secretly get power, or some other personal gain, at the expense of our brothers and sisters. On a large scale, many organizations exist today that are willing to inflict pain and suffering—and even death—in order to get ahead financially. Huge drug cartels use bribery, adultery, blackmail, and even murder to market a product that leads to even more misery and death.

Aside from secret combinations, otherwise respectable businessmen produce and advertise harmful products, such as tobacco and alcoholic beverages, that lead to much disease, numerous disabling accidents, and a tremendous number of deaths. An enormous amount of pain and suffering results directly from these two products alone.

Even though we may not be involved in large and prosperous organizations whose products lead to human suffering, we can all become susceptible to secret combinations, because these combinations begin in a person's heart. The moment people find themselves secretly desiring to gain power or wealth at the expense of someone else, a secret combination of sorts is born. First they combine with Satan, and then, many times, they include others in their plans. Secret combinations do not need to be large in order to cause great damage and suffering. Think of all the dishonesty and violence that is done by individuals working with Satan alone, and imagine how much better and happier the world would be if these minicombinations did not exist. Even better, think what the world would be like if everyone combined with God, instead of Satan, in doing things to help others succeed and be happy.

The desire for gain and power is opposite from the basic principles of the gospel. Many of us, at one time or another, are tempted to take advantage of someone in order to get ahead in the world. Through study and prayer and obedience, and with the Lord's help, we can overcome these selfish desires and become partners with God. The powerful effect the gospel can have when we allow it into our lives was demonstrated in the book of Helaman. Notice what the Lamanites did to destroy the Gadianton robbers and the secret combinations, which were causing much suffering in their lands: "And it came to pass that the Lamanites did hunt the band of robbers of Gadianton; and they did preach the word of God among the more wicked part of them, insomuch that this band of robbers was utterly destroyed from among the Lamanites" (Helaman 6:37).

As we open our hearts to the gospel, we become less and less inclined to take advantage of those around us, and we feel a greater desire to help others become successful and happy. We quickly come to experience the joy that results from unity, love, and brotherhood, and from being one with God.

Chapter 59

DO IT
WITH REAL INTENT

MORONI 7:5–11

Norway often has bitter, subzero temperatures in winter. One early-morning seminary teacher pedals his bike seven miles every morning in this subzero weather in order to reach his seminary class. His teenage daughter rides behind him except on days when it is so cold that he won't allow her to come. It is not difficult to guess this teacher's motives—only love for his students and for the gospel would be motivation enough for him to give this kind of service.

Our motives, intentions, and desires are most important in our Church service and in all religious acts that we perform. Mormon said that "a bitter fountain cannot bring forth good water" (Moroni 7:11), meaning that our motives have to be right in order for us to accomplish what God wants us to do. Mormon also stated: "For behold, God hath said a man being evil cannot do that which is good; for if he offereth a gift, or prayeth unto God, except he shall do it with real intent it profiteth him nothing. For behold, it is not counted unto him for righteousness." (Moroni 7:6–7.)

It is not counted as righteousnesss because his motives and desires are wrong. When our motives are wrong we are not serving God or others, but we are serving ourselves in some way. The scriptures refer to this type of service as "priestcrafts." The Lord gave Nephi a commandment that not only defined priestcrafts but emphasized some of the right reasons for service in the kingdom of God:

> He [the Lord] commandeth that there shall be no priest-crafts; for, behold, priestcrafts are that men preach and set themselves up for a light unto the world, that they may get gain and praise of the world; but they seek not the welfare of Zion.
>
> Behold, the Lord hath forbidden this thing; wherefore, the Lord God hath given a commandment that all men should have charity, which charity is love. . . . Wherefore, if they should have charity they would not suffer the laborer in Zion to perish.
>
> But the laborer in Zion shall labor for Zion; for if they labor for money they shall perish. (2 Nephi 26:29–31.)

We did not come to this earth just to *do* but to *become*—to become like God, and eventually to become gods ourselves. We are never more like God than when we serve unselfishly, out of love for God and for those around us. This same principle applies to church attendance and to all other forms of our religious worship. When we attend church out of duty or because we are commanded, we obtain some blessings; but when we attend out of love for God and with a desire to worship and to learn of him, we receive strength and peace, and we enjoy great spiritual growth.

When we serve or speak or participate in the kingdom of God for social reasons or for the attention we receive or because it gives us an opportunity to display our talents, our motives are poor. In fact, we may be meeting the criteria for priestcrafts—to preach for the "gain and praise of the world." When we give service humbly and prayerfully for the benefit of those we have been called to serve, the Lord pours out his Spirit upon us and touches the hearts of those we serve.

Our motives when praying are just as important as our motives in the other areas of our private and public worship. Mormon said: "And likewise also is it counted evil unto a man, if he shall pray and not with real intent of heart; yea, and it profiteth him nothing, for God receiveth none such" (Moroni 7:9).

Motives may be the reason why some receive joy in their service and others do not. They may be the reason why many feel the Spirit in a meeting while others just watch the time. Motives determine whether our prayers become real communication with God rather than mere words that seem to hang in the air and then tumble back to the ground. Motives are the difference between real religious worship and just going through the motions. One is a living, growing thing, while the other is unrewarding and unfulfilling. To serve for the right reasons is to serve for the reasons Christ served. This kind of service benefits both the giver and the receiver.

Chapter 60

CHARITY
NEVER FAILETH

MORONI 7:44–48

The ancient Greek language, from which the New Testament was translated, had three separate words for *love*: *eros, philos,* and *agape. Agape* is the word used, in the Greek text, in passages in which Christ speaks of love. *Agape* is love for those who have done nothing to deserve our love. It is love given unconditionally. This is the kind of love that Jesus demonstrated and which is referred to as *charity* in the scriptures. Mormon described this kind of love:

> And if a man be meek and lowly in heart, and confesses by the power of the Holy Ghost that Jesus is the Christ, he must needs have charity; for if he have not charity he is nothing; wherefore he must needs have charity.
>
> And charity suffereth long, and is kind, and envieth not, and is not puffed up, seeketh not her own, is not easily provoked, thinketh no evil, and rejoiceth not in iniquity but rejoiceth in the truth, beareth all things, believeth all things, hopeth all things, endureth all things. (Moroni 7:44–45.)

When we have charity we strive to do what is best for those around us. This love is not given partially or just on certain occasions, but it is given freely in all circumstances because it has become part of our personality and character. Charity is love that is completely impartial. When we possess charity, which is the pure love of Christ, we love others as Christ loved them. Our love is not limited by race, belief, or economic status. We even love our enemies and care for their welfare as much as we care for the welfare of our friends. This kind of love is spontaneous. It is not given out of duty or to fulfill some commandment, but it is a natural expression of the way that we feel.

When we possess this great gift of charity we are concerned about each individual. This kind of love for each person was demonstrated by an Elder Nolan Bergeson. He was a quiet, reserved missionary who was serious about helping the people he served. While visiting a branch of the Church he became acquainted with a woman who was deaf and could not speak but who still attended church. For many years she had expressed her desire to be baptized, but a mission rule said she had to be taught all six missionary lessons before baptism. Since none of the missionaries knew sign language, she had never been taught the lessons.

Elder Bergeson obtained a card that had the signs of the alphabet on it. In a six-hour marathon he taught her the first discussion, spelling each word to her and having her spell back the answers to each of his questions. Elder Bergeson was not satisfied with this approach, so he went to the library and found some books on sign language. He practiced continually, and each discussion became easier and more rewarding for both Elder Bergeson and this faithful woman. The last discussion did not take much more time than a normal discussion would. After many years of waiting and praying, this woman was finally baptized into the kingdom of God, and to this day she praises and blesses the name of Elder Bergeson in her unspoken language. Because he possessed the gift of charity, Elder Bergeson felt a concern for every child of God. (See Steven A. Wolfe, *Ensign*, August 1978, p. 66.)

Charity, like so many other important qualities, is a gift of God. As we prepare our hearts for this great gift, God fills our hearts with love. Mormon explained how to receive charity: "But charity is the pure love of Christ. . . . Wherefore, my beloved brethren, pray unto the Father with all the energy of heart, that ye may be filled with this love, which he hath bestowed upon all who are true followers of his Son, Jesus Christ; that ye may become the sons of God; that when he shall appear we shall be like him, for we shall see him as he is; that we may have this hope; that we may be purified even as he is pure. Amen." (Moroni 7:47–48.)

The bestowal of this love was demonstrated by a seminary

teacher who inherited a group of students who were difficult to teach. During the previous two years they had driven three teachers out of their classes and out of the seminary program, and they hadn't improved any during the summer. This teacher reached the point where he too was ready to quit teaching—and he was in the process of doing so when his supervisor said to him, "Do you know what the problem is? You don't love these students—you are only concerned about yourself!"

As the seminary teacher thought about this, he realized that it was true, and he decided to give teaching another chance. Some of his students were so obnoxious that he knew he could never come to love them on his own, so he pleaded with God to fill his heart with the pure love of Christ. It was a Sunday night when the miracle happened. As he knelt in prayer his feelings of discouragement and fear were swept away and replaced with feelings of confidence and love.

Within a few weeks nearly all of the students had begun responding to his love and were learning the gospel of Jesus Christ. Most of his discipline problems disappeared when he learned to care more about his students than about himself.

The possession of the gift of charity changes not only us but also those we come in contact with. One lady, who was referred to as an "eternal investigator" because she had heard the missionary lessons so many times, asked the missionaries why they continued to put up with constant persecution and ridicule, shrugged off their lack of success, and continued to teach the people in her area.

One of the missionaries looked her straight in the eye and said sincerely, "It is because we love you and the other people in this country." The spirit of the discussion was altered, the lady's heart was opened to the sweet Spirit of Christ, and she soon became a member of the Church.

As we strive to live the gospel of Jesus Christ and "pray unto the Father with all the energy of our hearts," he will bestow upon us the gift of charity, one of the most valuable and important gifts we will ever receive. As we respond to this gift and reach out to others, this love will actually increase within our hearts. It will not only enrich our own lives but will improve and enhance the lives of those we come in contact with.

Chapter 61

TRUTH
OF ALL THINGS

MORONI 10:3–5

One of the first steps of spiritual growth and of coming to a knowledge of the truthfulness of the gospel was outlined by Moroni: "Behold, I would exhort you that when ye shall read these things . . . ye would remember how merciful the Lord hath been unto the children of men, from the creation of Adam even down until the time that ye shall receive these things, and ponder it in your hearts" (Moroni 10:3).

Moroni was talking about coming to know the truthfulness of the Book of Mormon, but his counsel also applies to receiving gospel truths from all sources. The love and mercy of God and Christ are the heart and soul of the gospel. As we ponder their great love, as demonstrated by the Atonement and in other ways, we prepare our hearts to receive the Holy Ghost. Knowing God's love for us gives us the confidence to pray and ask him for the things we need and desire.

Moroni went on to say: "And when ye shall receive these things, I would exhort you that ye would ask God, the Eternal Father, in the name of Christ, if these things are not true; and if ye shall ask with a sincere heart, with real intent, having faith in Christ, he will manifest the truth of it unto you, by the power of the Holy Ghost. And by the power of the Holy Ghost ye may know the truth of all things." (Moroni 10:4–5.)

God has promised to give a spiritual witness to anyone who qualifies. Each of us has to meet the requirements in order to receive a witness. To give a witness to a person who is not prepared would be more harmful than helpful. One of the requirements is to pray with a sincere heart and with real intent. If we are sincere, we are willing to do whatever is necessary to qualify. We need to desire more than just to *know* the truth—we must desire to *live* the truth before God will reveal it to us.

It was Joseph Smith's desire for truth that led him into the woods to pray. This special day had been preceded by much searching and prayer. He had read the scriptures and had attended other churches. He had spent much time in thought and in pondering and pleading for direction. When he knelt in the Sacred Grove, his heart was right. He desired not just to know the truth but to serve God with all of his heart and mind and might. His prayers were answered because he was sincere and because his intentions were pure. His prayers were answered because he was willing to pay the price.

When we have the same desire to know and live the truth that Joseph did, we too will receive answers to our prayers. But it takes more than just prayer alone. In 1989 a jetliner filled with passengers was crossing the Pacific Ocean when a huge tear opened on one side of the plane. Nine people were sucked through the hole to their deaths, and the lives of the other passengers were in serious jeopardy. After having landed the plane safely back in Honolulu, the captain was asked what he did when the plane ripped open. The captain replied, "I prayed, then went to work." (See Thomas S. Monson, *Ensign*, May 1989, p. 44.)

This is about the best advice we can receive on how to gain a witness of the Book of Mormon or of any other gospel truth. We must pray and then go to work. The promise is sure. As we do our part the Lord will do his part, and through the witness of the Holy Ghost we will gain the assurance that we need. As we follow through and make these truths an integral part of the way we think and live, we will receive an even greater witness, and our testimonies will become even stronger and firmer than before.

INDEX